MIRACLE AT SEA

Miracle at Sea

The Sinking of the *Zamzam* and Our Family's Rescue

Blessings in our Lord.

Eleanor Anderson

Eleanor Danielson Anderson

Quiet Waters Publications
Bolivar, Missouri
2001

For information contact:
    Quiet Waters Publications
    P.O. Box 34, Bolivar, MO 65613-0034.
    E-mail: QWP@usa.net.

For prices and order information visit:
    http://www.quietwaterspub.com
    http://www.quietwaterspub.com/*Zamzam*

Cover: This photo of the *Zamzam* was copied by V. Eugene
Johnson from a British magazine.

Back cover: Mrs. Danielson with her six children on board
the *Zamzam*. For more than a month Mr. Danielson, who
worked as a missionary in Tanganyika, did not know whether
his family was still alive (photo by V. Eugene Johnson, courtesy of the Evangelical Lutheran Church in America Ar-
chives).

1st edition 2000
2nd revised edition 2001

ISBN 1-931475-05-9

Dedicated with love and appreciation to the marriage partners of us Danielson children: Jean, Carl, Ray, Jim, Marilyn, and Dave

CONTENTS

PREFACE

Before writing *MIRACLE AT SEA,* Eleanor Danielson Anderson has fascinated and moved audiences with her oral account of the sinking of the *Zamzam* in the shark-infested waters of the mid-Atlantic. The book also holds a tribute to Lillian Danielson, Eleanor's mother, whose calm faith and quiet common sense kept her six children alive during the harrowing thirty days aboard the *Dresden,* a German prison ship. The *Dresden* had to plow through the British Blockade to bring its precious cargo, including more than 120 American missionaries, safely to a harbor in German-occupied France.

My father, Ralph Hult, was one of those missionaries who survived the sinking of the *Zamzam.* He was in the same shell-ridden lifeboat with Mrs. Danielson and her six children on the morning of April 17th, 1941. Their story and the stories of the other survivors became front-page news throughout the world, when the sinking of the *Zamzam* was announced a month later.

MIRACLE AT SEA is also a love story between husband and wife, as well as between a mother and her brave children. Lillian Danielson's tender love and devotion for her husband and her six young children, as well as her deep, abiding faith in God, will move you to tears, while, at the same time, it will bring you great joy.

Ingrid Trobisch-Youngdale

ACKNOWLEDGMENTS

Although it has been nearly sixty years since the *Zamzam* went to the bottom of the ocean, the drama and faith surrounding that event still stirs my heart. Audiences, too, seemed to be moved by God's miraculous care. It is a story to be shared and treasured, for it shows how faith in God can wrap us in His matchless love and help us endure the trials and disappointments life brings.

For some time now, God has been nudging me: "Write down for the coming generation what the Lord has done, so that people not yet born will praise him." (Psalm 102:18 TEV)

Finally, I have responded.

While at the age of nine I was old enough to remember the *Zamzam* experience firsthand, I have also turned to others' reports to supplement my memories: the 1941 *Zamzam* book published by the Augustana Synod, various magazine articles, and our family's scrapbook. However, it is Mother's own personal account upon which I have relied most heavily. In a lengthy report written for us children in 1946, Mother shared the many homey, personal details which this book includes. Her writing also clearly expresses her faith in our Heavenly Father and her love for Dad and us children.

There are many other family members to whom I am greatly indebted, and to them I express my sincere thanks: to all my brothers and sisters for their permission to write about them; to my own children, Peter, John, James, Mary, and Paul, who have supported my role as *Zamzam* storyteller throughout the years; to my grandchildren, stepchildren, special nieces, and other family members and friends, who have given encouragement as well; and most of all to my husband, Carl, for his endless patience and support during the writing process.

In addition, I am deeply grateful to Ingrid Trobisch-Youngdale, Stephen Trobisch, and David Trobisch, of Quiet Waters Publications, for making this project become a reality. Their personal encouragement and expertise have truly been a gift.

Above all, I give thanks to God.

Eleanor Anderson

ONE
The Big Question

The jingling telephone downstairs disturbed the nighttime quietness in our little home in Lindsborg, Kansas. It was nearly ten o'clock, the last day of February, 1941.

Throwing aside the heavy quilt and grabbing her old chenille robe, Mother headed toward the stairs. Who would be calling so late at night? With Dad on the other side of the globe, it was easy to imagine news of an accident or a serious illness. 'Heavenly Father, please don't let it be bad news about my sweetheart,' Mother prayed as she hurried down the steps.

Reaching for the phone on the kitchen wall, Mother answered cautiously, "Hello. Hello. Yes, this is Lillian Danielson speaking..."

Laurence, the oldest of us six children, had heard the phone, too. He stumbled sleepily into the hall and plunked himself down on the top step, straining to hear what Mother was saying. 'After all, it's my job to look after Mama,' he told himself. Indeed, though he was only ten-and-a-half years of age, Laurence was man of the house ever since Dad had returned to the mission field in East Africa last summer. Now, giving a shudder in the wintry night chill and wishing he had draped a blanket around his shoulders, Laurence waited anxiously, unable to make out a word Mother was saying. The minutes seemed like hours.

Soon, however, Mother trekked back up the stairs, her dark eyes beaming with joy. With a new excitement in her voice, Mother urged Laurence, "Sonny, come to my room. We need to talk. And perhaps the older girls should come too."

The older girls were myself, Eleanor, almost nine years old, and Evelyn, seven-and-a-half. Barely awake, we stumbled into Mother's room. There was no need to summon Luella, four-and-a-half, and Lois, one-and-a-half, for they shared Mother's room. Rubbing their sleepy eyes and yawning, they sat up in bed and looked around, wondering what the commotion was all about.

"Mama, I am going to get Wilfred. He should not be left out," Laurence announced abruptly, returning soon with our three-year-old brother.

Now, with all six children gathered around her, Mother began to explain the phone call. "That was Dr. Swanson from the mission board, kiddies. He wants to know if we would like to go to Africa soon and be with Daddy."

The words were hardly spoken before we joined in a spontaneous chorus of "Yes! Yes! Yeah!" Now wide-awake, little Luella jumped and clapped, and Wilfred started to bounce on the bed. Even baby Lois seemed to catch the mood, chiming in with a loud "Daddy! Daddy!"

"But Mama, how will we get there?" Evelyn asked when the cheering had quieted down.

"Dr. Swanson says a ship named *Zamzam* is sailing soon. Many missionaries will be traveling on the *Zamzam*, and Daddy has asked if we can come with them," Mother answered. She did not need to explain more about Dad's inquiry. We older children remembered very well how our family had left Tanganyika (Tanzania), East Africa, in May of 1939 to come to the States on furlough. Our baby sister, Lois, had been born soon after our arrival in Lindsborg, our furlough home.

In May of 1940, our whole family had been ready to return to Africa; passage was booked on an ocean liner and trunks packed. World War II, however, had begun. Each day's news brought troubling reports of growing uncertainty and restrictions abroad. In the face of such turmoil, our family's travel plans were canceled, and we settled down in Lindsborg again.

The war had also caused a critical shortage of missionaries on the field, and Dad was desperately needed back in Tanganyika. He found no peace in his soul. Should he go back alone? Mother understood Dad's dilemma. Talking, praying, and even weeping in each other's arms, they had struggled to know and follow God's will. We older children, too, had been brought into the discussions and prayers. Finally, with the family's support, Dad had volunteered to return to Africa alone for a shortened term or until the family could join him.

So, on a hot Kansas day in late July, 1940, Dad had left for Africa. In three days, Baby Lois would be one year old, and Laurence had just turned ten. It was a heart-wrenching fare-well, but also a good-bye blessed with God's peace. Traveling by way of the Pacific, Dad had reached Tanganyika safely and had taken up his missionary duties. Though the war in Europe had intensified, the United States had not yet entered the conflict.

Now, seven months after Dad left, we learned that we might soon join him in Africa.

"What did you tell Dr. Swanson?" Laurence asked.

Mother looked at the trusting faces of her six children. She chose her words carefully. "I told Dr. Swanson we need to pray before we make such a big decision. We want to do God's will, not ours. He will help us decide."

"But Mama, you said there is not much time," I interrupted. "How long can Dr. Swanson wait?"

Mother hesitated. "I told him I would send our answer to-morrow." That did not leave much time for prayer. The *Zamzam* was scheduled to sail from New York on March 11th, and today was February 28th. Dr. Swanson had less than two weeks to obtain the necessary visa, which must come from Tanganyika. But before he could do that, he needed to know if we were willing to travel at this time.

The answer was obvious. Tanganyika had been the place of birth and childhood for most of us children, and we were ea-ger to return. As for Mother, she longed to be back there again with her husband, Elmer, serving as a missionary wife and mother.

However, Mother knew we must follow God's desires, not

our own; we needed to talk it over with our Heavenly Father. We knelt beside Mother's bed and took turns praying aloud. Even Baby Lois joined in, repeating a strong "Ah-men!" after each prayer, sometimes causing us older children to snicker. Even Mother could not keep from smiling.

But when Wilfred prayed, Mother felt a lump in her throat. She would never forget last summer's farewell when Dad had left for Africa. Wilfred had jumped into Dad's arms and clung to him. The tears rolled down Dad's cheeks, as he had to unwrap his little son's trusting arms and forcefully place him back down on the floor. Wilfred's weeping had been inconsolable as Dad climbed into the waiting car and faded from sight. Now Wilfred prayed hopefully, "Jesus, help us go to Daddy. We go see Daddy now. I wear my red cap. Amen."

When prayers were finished, little Luella snuggled close and gave Mother a kiss on the cheek, saying, "That kiss is from me." Then she planted another tender kiss on the other cheek. "That one is from Daddy. I know he wants us to come. He misses me. And he misses you, too, Mama."

Mother's eyes moistened with tears. 'God has so richly blessed me.' She sent us off to bed again, tucking in Luella and Lois beside her. It did not take long for the little ones to drift off to sleep again.

TWO
Night of Pondering

Mother could not go to sleep quickly. Her mind was filled with thoughts of the trip, which would bring her to her sweetheart. How she wished we were already there!

Mother's thoughts also flew back to the memories of years gone by. Born in 1899, the ninth of ten children of Nels and Amalia Larson, she had grown up on the family farm in southeastern Kansas. Nels and Amalia were immigrants from Sweden, devout Christians who lived their faith day by day. Mother's earliest memories included the horse and buggy rides to the little Lutheran church in Vilas, near Chanute. How good it had felt to be in church. No matter where she was, however, Mother had been blessed with the assurance that God was near, and He loved her personally.

Her own beloved mother had died during the 1918 flu epidemic. Mother had taught country school and kept house for her father and brothers before attending Bethany Academy and College in Lindsborg, Kansas. God had already touched her heart with the call to be a missionary, but it was during college years that the call became certain. To prepare for pioneer missionary service, Mother attended Bible School and a few months of nurses' training after graduating from Bethany.

The commissioning service had been held at the Vilas church in September, 1928. Mother still felt a sense of awe that God would call her—a humble and rather shy girl from a Kansas farm—to serve in far-away Africa. Deep in her heart, though, she knew that God had called her.

She still felt pain as she remembered how hard it had been

to say good-bye to her aging father, realizing that she would probably never see him again on earth. And so it was—a heart attack took him three years after she left for Africa.

Friends and family members had tried desperately to talk her out of leaving: "Africa is so far away. Nobody knows much about Africa. Will you be safe? Aren't you worried about all the diseases?"

Others said to her: "You'll never get married or have children. Have you considered that?" Mother's beautiful face was framed by dark brown hair—she was indeed an attractive woman. Several young men had wanted to marry her, but she had firmly turned them away. She knew God wanted her in Africa, even if it meant never getting married. God had a marvelous surprise in store, however.

Mother's heart still fluttered whenever she thought about how she had met Dad on the ship en route to Africa in 1928. Dad, a newly ordained pastor from Connecticut, was both single and strikingly handsome. Like Mother, he had felt God's call to be a missionary and was being sent by the Augustana Lutheran Synod to the pioneer work among the Iramba people in central Tanganyika. Right from the beginning, it seemed Mother and Dad were meant for each other.

As the long ocean voyage neared its end, they had stood alone at the ship's railing, Dad tenderly professing his love. He was absolutely convinced that Mother was the answer to his prayers for a life-long companion.

Mother remembered how she had longed for Dad's embrace, but she did not allow it. 'Is this true love or just a temporary attraction?' she asked herself. 'And what about my contract with the mission board?'

Finally, Mother and Dad arrived on the mission field, where they took daily language classes together. No longer could Mother deny or hide her love for Dad. Before long, they announced, "God seems to be telling us we can serve Him better as a married couple than we can by remaining single."

And so it was that Mother and Dad were married on August 15th, 1929, in the little chapel at the Ruruma Mission Station.

The simple ceremony and joyous celebration was the first Christian wedding among the Iramba people.

The wedding bells in Mother's heart had never stopped ringing. She and Dad were true sweethearts. But both never forgot that their relationship to Christ and His Kingdom's work came first and foremost. That is how they could endure being separated now for a season.

'But does God really mean for me to go to Elmer at this time?' Mother contemplated, as she lay awake during the long night hours following the phone call. 'Should I uproot the children now in the middle of a school year? And I am sure, if Elmer knew how soon the *Zamzam* would be sailing, he would not have expected us to get ready on such short notice. But, I can manage.' The difficulty would be for Dr. Swanson to get the visa in time, since overseas communication was slow.

Another troubling thought was the war. Even though the United States was not involved, Mother wondered about the safety of travel for Americans. Then she remembered that Dr. Swanson had said that the *Zamzam* is a neutral, Egyptian ship. It would avoid the European war zone, traveling by way of South America and South Africa. Nearly a hundred fifty missionaries would be traveling on the *Zamzam*. Mission boards would not be sending their missionaries on a ship they did not consider safe.

Bit by bit, as Mother remembered God's astonishing involvement in her past years and as she wrestled with the gigantic decision before her, God gave His answer: 'Yes! Now is God's time for you to go to Africa with the children. As He has been with you in the past, God will be with you now. Trust in Him.'

Filled with a newfound peace, Mother finally fell asleep.

THREE
No Time to Waste

Even though the next morning was Saturday, we children got up early. Mother, hearing our chatter as she awakened, wondered for a moment why the night had seemed so short. Then, like a flash, it came back to her: the telephone call, the family discussion, and the long night hours of remembering and praying. Now wide-awake, her heart turned again to God. 'Thank you, Lord, for this new day. Bless and keep Elmer. Guide us today as we answer Dr. Swanson's call about going to Africa.'

Quickly pulling her dark brown hair into a bun and donning her chenille robe, Mother hurried down to the kitchen and started cooking oatmeal. She could sense an air of quiet excitement as we gathered at the breakfast table.

Little Luella snuggled in Mother's arms for a morning hug before asking the big question: "Mama, are we going?" All eyes were on Mother as she filled our cereal bowls and led in table prayer.

Then she looked around the table at our questioning faces and cleared her throat, "First, do any of you have something you want to say?" Nobody said a thing, so Mother continued, slowly, solemnly, "Well, kiddies, I have been thinking and praying much of the night. It does seem God is telling us to go on the *Zamzam*. I'll send the telegram to Dr. Swanson today." We all smiled in approval. "But let's not tell anyone yet," Mother cautioned. "We might not be able to go, if Dr. Swanson cannot get the visa in time. Don't get your hopes too high." Mother was sorry to dampen our eagerness, but we needed to be reminded of the uncertainty surrounding our situation.

We talked some more. Then, clearing the table, Mother continued, "Remember, today is the day I am going to McPherson for the district Women's Missionary Society meeting. So, be good and get your chores done while I am gone. Don't forget to feed the chickens, Sonny, and give them fresh water." Then, looking at all three of us older children, Mother added tenderly, "Most important of all, take good care of the little ones. And be sure to dress Lois warm—it's quite chilly today." As usual, Mother felt a bit guilty leaving us, but she knew she could trust us to look out for one another.

Mother hurried upstairs to get dressed. Before long, a blue Chevy pulled to a stop outside our Lindsborg home at 133 North Pine Street, and Mother climbed in the back seat, joining her friends for the fourteen-mile ride to McPherson, Kansas.

The women chatted about how eagerly they awaited spring on this March 1st, and what a fine meditation Pastor Olson had given the previous Wednesday night, and how well the high school orchestra had performed in concert last night. Mother joined in the conversation in her usual quiet way, giving no hint of the amazing new plans and thoughts that were swirling through her mind. Silently, she marveled at how God was already at work in the unfolding drama, for at lunch time she planned to slip away from the women's meeting and walk to the County Court House to do her part in applying for the visa and validating our passports.

Although the women's morning meeting was inspiring and well-prepared, Mother found it hard to concentrate. Lunchtime came at last. She simply told her friends she had an errand to run and would be back soon. Reaching the courthouse, Mother discovered that the clerk's office was closed at noon on Saturdays. It would not open until Monday morning.

Mother was not deterred. She called the clerk at his home. When Mother explained the urgency of the matter, the clerk graciously returned to the office to complete the required paper work.

After the telegram to Dr. Swanson was sent, Mother hurried back to the church for the rest of the meeting. Her friends had no idea of what Mother had accomplished during the lunch hour. She kept it a secret. God knew. That was enough for now.

As the Chevy hummed along Route 81 back to Lindsborg, a prayer of thanks filled Mother's heart. The first step of the journey had been taken.

'Now, where do I begin? How did we ever accumulate so much?' Mother asked herself. Things had been ready for the family's intended return to Africa last May, but clothes and toys and books and letters had filled the drawers and closets again since then. Sorting a drawer here, setting up boxes there, Mother began putting things in trunks and suitcases.

"But Mama, what if we do not go to Africa? Then all this work is wasted," she was reminded again and again by one of us children.

"I know. But we have to work and plan as if it will happen and then just leave it in God's Hands."

The packing was only one part of the preparations. What should be done with the live chickens, the jars of canned goods in the cellar, and the meat in the freezer locker? The house would need to be emptied and ready for renters, except for the south bedroom, which Mother had decided to use for storage of our things.

On that first Tuesday after the call, Mother worked late into the night. A trunk and boxes by her side, she began clearing the first floor closet. As she sorted and packed, an overwhelming wave of doubt came over her. 'It is just too much! It cannot be done. I just cannot handle this all by myself. I wish Elmer were here...' Mother had been holding so much inside. She needed a good cry. Her eyes filling with tears, she walked to the sofa and got down on her knees. Then she buried her head in her arms and let the sobs come. She felt so weary and helpless.

Then it was as if she could hear God's promise: 'When you are weak, I am strong. Lean on me.' For a while, Mother just rested, quietly, in silence, letting God fill her with His promised strength. Then, renewed and at peace again, Mother rose to her feet and returned to the sorting and packing.

The next day, March 5th, a telegram came from Dr. Swanson: "Can't obtain visa in time. You must wait." Mother's heart sank. The news came like a deathblow. No trip. No being with her sweetheart again soon. All this effort wasted. Trying to put aside the painful disappointment, Mother told herself she could understand the situation. No one could be blamed. Dr. Swanson had been doing all he could, even enlisting the help of Congressman Youngdahl. There simply was not enough time before the sailing date.

Mother broke the news to us children. "Maybe this news is God's will, kiddies," she said weakly, trying to console us. At the same time, Mother had felt so certain that God meant for us to travel on the *Zamzam*. Had she been wrong?

The next day brought sudden, soaring hope. A telegram from the shipping company reported that the *Zamzam*'s sailing would be delayed until March 19th. Immediately Mother sent a telegram to Dr. Swanson, encouraging him to keep trying. Dr. Swanson wired back that he would try, but "doubt it possible."

Undaunted, Mother returned to packing in earnest. As yet, our plans were still a family secret. In the second week, Mother decided to confide in Pastor Olson and also in the women's prayer group. The women were quite surprised, but they seemed understanding.

Furthermore, the women said they would help Mother and so would their husbands. Ellen came over to help with the laundry and mending. "And don't worry about your chickens, Lillian. Willie will take care of selling them if you go."

Judith was good at schedules and business details. "I can cancel your subscriptions and the music lessons," she offered. "And Bernard will take care of paying bills and renting the house."

Another friend, also named Lillian, began sending over meals and snacks. "Then you can concentrate on the packing." Alice sent over food as well.

That second week of March was speeding by. In order to arrive in New York City by train on the 18th, Mother figured that the very latest the family would need to leave Lindsborg was Sunday, March 16th. By Friday morning, the 14th, there was still no news of the needed visa. "We still have two days," Mother reminded us at breakfast. "Kiddies, I am going to shop in Salina today. If we are going to be gone for four or five years, we will need more underwear and socks and shoes." Perhaps it was foolish, but Mother was not ready to give up. Every hour now counted.

Mother looked at me: "Eleanor, would you stay home from school today and watch the younger trio?" I nodded, proud to be designated "little mama" for the day.

Mother rushed to catch the nine o'clock bus to Salina, twenty miles north of Lindsborg. All day, she hurried in and out of department stores, calculating sizes and future needs, purchasing as reasonably as possible.

At home, I dutifully watched over Luella, Wilfred, and Lois. When Laurence and Evelyn arrived home from school, all six of us gathered in the kitchen for a snack. We munched on cookies and chatted and giggled. Our big secret bonded us with an unusual sense of being family. "Guess what," Laurence announced brashly. "If we go on the *Zamzam*, I won't have to write spelling words a hundred times for Monday. I got a lot wrong on the test today." We giggled some more.

Then we heard a car stop out front. Mr. Esping hurried toward our house. He was carrying a yellow "Western Union" envelope. "It's a telegram," Laurence gasped. Would the message be what we hoped for? Moments later Laurence read with a loud voice, "Visa will await you in New York."

Instantly, we hugged and twirled and clapped and squealed, "We're going! We're going! We're going to Africa, to Daddy!"

We were so eager to tell Mother, we could hardly contain

ourselves as we awaited her return. Minutes seemed like hours. "When will Mama get home? When is she coming?" We kept looking up the street.

Finally, we saw her, wearily trudging up State Street, laden with packages. Running to meet her, we yelled excitedly, "It came! It came! The telegram came! We can go! He got the visa!"

Tears trickled down Mother's cheeks, tears of absolute gratitude and joy: 'Thank you, Father.'

FOUR
Leaving Lindsborg

Mother shivered in the early morning chill as she knelt beside her bed in prayer. A few minutes later, she was in the kitchen stirring oatmeal. Her calmness belied her excitement—this was our family's last day in Lindsborg. It was Saturday, March 15th, 1941.

Despite of all her tireless work the past two weeks, there was still much to do before leaving for Africa. "I need to get to the dentist one more time, kiddies, but first I am going to send a telegram to Uncle Oscar. I hope he can drive us to Vilas tomorrow." Without her saying so, we knew that Mother longed to spend a few farewell hours with her brothers and families and step-mother Sophie. "And then we could get on the train in Chanute," Mother added.

A little later, Oscar telephoned. "I am going to drive up this afternoon. I ought to get to Lindsborg by four or so. I imagine you can use some strong arms to move the furniture. Don't you try lifting anything heavy yourself, Lillie." Mother smiled, feeling comfort in hearing her big brother call her "Lillie" again.

Mother found it harder and harder to stay with the work herself, as one friend after another came to say good-bye. The news of our impending departure had spread throughout the community. Margaret Peterson's dad brought over a small package for Mother to take to his daughter, a nurse in Tanganyika, and, when Mr. Peterson saw how much work remained, he rolled up his sleeves and pitched right in, moving furniture. Other friends offered to run errands. Some came back with snacks for the train ride.

Pastor Olson's wife called to invite us to the parsonage for supper. "And why not let Laurence spend the night with Roger?" Soon, others also offered places for sleeping that final night.

Children responded to the news as well. Shortly after noon, the Pine Street neighborhood kids came in a group, almost a dozen of them, gathering on our front porch. Shyly, we Danielson children opened the door and gazed out at our buddies, now solemn and a bit bewildered by what was happening. Martha Jane held a large envelope. "Here! Read a message every day, just to remember us. It's from all of us," she explained, as she thrust a packet of letters toward Laurence.

Laurence took the envelope, hoping nobody noticed the tear about to roll down his cheek. "Thank you. We'll miss you," he murmured, thinking of all the hours spent together playing softball and "kick the can." It was hard to say goodbye. Finally, in awkward silence, the group meandered away, and Laurence slowly closed the door.

After our pals left, I suggested, "Let's go to the school now and pick up our things." With the help of the janitor, Laurence, Evelyn, and I were given access to our classrooms. Somberly, we cleared out our desks. Then, using our best penmanship and grammar, we wrote farewell notes, leaving them on our teachers' desks.

With each passing hour, our departure was becoming more real. "I feel sad about saying goodbye—even though I do want to go to Africa," I told Mother. She knew what I meant, for the day was overflowing with mixed emotions for her, too. Lindsborg friends were so dear and farewells so hard, but waiting for her in Africa were her sweetheart and the missionary work. She must keep looking forward, she told herself.

Oscar arrived in the late afternoon. He was soon busy with the man-sized jobs yet to be done. Then it was time for supper with the Olsons, a tasty meal of meat loaf and scalloped potatoes. But Mother appreciated even more the spiritual nourishment she received as Pastor Olson led in devotions, focusing on God's promise, "Lo, I am with you always." That promise had always spoken to Mother's soul, but it took on new meaning now as she faced the tremendous challenge of traveling to Africa with six young children, without the help of her beloved Elmer and in the shadow of the escalating war.

Returning from supper, the phone rang again. It was Mrs. Pihlblad, wife of the college president. "My husband and I stopped by to say good-bye, but you weren't home. So we will say good-bye now on the phone. You are a brave woman, Mrs. Danielson. God be with you." Mother felt both humbled and strengthened. She knew she would never forget the love and support the Lindsborg community had shown her this day.

A couple of hours later, the Olsons came to pick up Laurence for the night. As he was going out the door, he turned around. "Mama, I won't see this house again for many years. I want to walk through the rooms just one more time." In a few minutes, Laurence came out of the house and, without looking back, solemnly climbed into the waiting car. Next, Evelyn went to spend the night with her best friend, Charlotte Ternstrom.

When the Hoffs came to pick up Luella and me, Luella hesitated, her little hand firmly clutching Mother's skirt. Giving Luella a long hug, Mother assured, "You'll be all right, dear. I will see you in the morning. You go with Eleanor now." Reluctantly, little Luella took my hand, holding back her tears as she tried to be brave for her Mama's sake.

Sensing how hard it had been for Luella to leave home, Mother was thankful she had decided that Wilfred and Lois would stay with her at our house that night, even if it meant they slept on blankets on the floor. They fell asleep quite easily, despite the activity around them.

Mother and Oscar worked steadily, quietly, into the night hours. By two-thirty in the morning, Mother urged Oscar to lie down and rest. "I won't stop working unless you do, Lillie," Oscar countered. So Mother, too, stretched out on the living room floor and relaxed.

However, just as soon as she heard Oscar snoring, Mother got up and resumed packing. At last she turned the key on the last suitcase and finished filling the carry-on bags. Dawn was starting to break. Mother had not slept a wink.

Oscar stirred and was soon on his feet again. In the faint light of early morning, he started loading the pick-up truck. Neighbor Albin Anderson helped with the heaviest trunks and suitcases. On top of the luggage, they piled Laurence's bike, two tricycles, and the green leather folding baby buggy, all covered by a canvas tarp. Mother felt so thankful for Oscar and Albin's help. "I could never have managed without you," she told them gratefully.

Glancing back to take a final look at our house at 133 North Pine, Mother climbed into the truck's cab, baby Lois sleeping in her arms and Wilfred hanging onto her coat, close beside her. Oscar took the driver's seat. With only two tries, the cold motor sputtered and turned, and the truck moved slowly up the street.

First Evelyn was picked up, then Laurence. Like good sports, they climbed into the back of the truck, in between the luggage, partly sheltered by the tarp. There would be space for me there. When the truck pulled up at Hoffs to pick up Luella and me, Mrs. Hoff urged, "Come in for a few minutes. I have hot cereal all ready."

Before long, breakfast was finished and Mother and the younger trio squeezed together in the cab of the truck. Luella snuggled contentedly, grateful to be back with her precious Mama. And there sat Wilfred, wearing his red knit cap, happily explaining, "I wear my cap. I go to see Daddy."

Helping us older three children climb into the back of the truck, Oscar reminded, "Tap on the window if you need help." We had a long, cold, cramped ride ahead.

Oscar took his place at the wheel, and soon the truck began to move again. The sun was just rising over the eastern horizon. The Bethany Church steeple, the railroad tracks, the grain elevators, and then the last City Limit sign were left behind. With a lump in her throat, Mother lifted her heart in prayer. We were on our way to Africa.

FIVE
Journey to New York

It was a long ride to Vilas. At Oscar's urging, Mother soon dropped off to sleep, with the three little children slumbering on her lap and beside her in the crowded cab. Awakening before long, Mother turned to see us three older children, riding in the back of the truck, bravely trying to smile, our faces taut with cold. It nearly broke her heart. "Oscar, we need to stop a few minutes, so the children can get warmed." Oscar understood, and soon he was able to pull off the highway at a service station.

We made several such stops en route to Vilas, extending the trip to more than six hours instead of only four. Finally, cold and weary, we arrived at Oscar's home, where the rest of the Larsons living in the Vilas area had gathered. Lovingly, they embraced us, remarking about how we children had grown and asking about the latest news from Dad.

But there was also a mood of serious doubt and grave concern. "I sure don't envy you your journey, Lillie," Aunt Anna said. "Do you really think it is wise?"

Silently Mother reminded herself that her family had always worried about her going to Africa, and she truly loved them for caring so much. She answered sweetly, "Thank you for caring; I do appreciate it. I know you are concerned. However, I believe God wants us to make this trip, and He has promised to be with us at all times. I will send you a cable as soon as we arrive in Africa." She paused and added, "Now, please excuse me for a few minutes; I need to make train arrangements."

Coming back from the phone, Mother reported good news:

"We can get to New York City in time if we leave Chanute tomorrow morning instead of tonight. But the agent suggested we get our tickets and check the luggage tonight, since we have so much." With the help of our uncles, the job was soon accomplished.

The long day was coming to a close. It was time for farewells and then a night of sleep. But first, Gust led in a touching prayer, committing us to the Heavenly Father's keeping. Once again, the Larsons' little sister Lillie was about to leave for far-away Africa.

"I want to sit by the window," several of us announced excitedly as we boarded the train Monday morning. Quickly Mother arranged that we take turns. And almost as quickly, she pulled out a bag of treats, quieting us while we adjusted to our new surroundings. We older children were soon fascinated watching the scenery whizzing by. Later, we busied ourselves with guessing games and entertaining the younger children. Mother even let us walk through several cars of the train. The younger trio stayed close to Mother; they needed supervision and help. Mother was thankful her youngest was not using diapers any longer, but still, it was a challenge to help "Little Miss Independence" attend to nature's call in a noisy restroom on a swaying, fast-moving train.

Mother was a gentle mother. She saw the good in us children and enjoyed our individual traits. Some might call her permissive, but she gave us a sense of freedom because she trusted us. As yet, we had not seriously disappointed her. As she sat there on the rolling train, she watched us with pride and contentment.

Others watched, too. Several paused and conversed as they passed through our coach. Some were curious about where this beautiful mother was going with six young children and unaccompanied by a husband. Mother explained briefly, but she sensed that most did not really understand what it meant to be a missionary.

Later that afternoon, one woman tapped Mother on the

shoulder and commented, "I can tell that you are a Christian mother as I see how you handle your children." Mother appreciated that word of encouragement and stored it in her heart for the days and weeks ahead.

The trip to New York meant changing trains only once, and that was in Chicago on Monday evening. That was no small task. Mother was thankful she could depend on us older children to help with the younger trio and all the assorted bags, as she led us into the huge waiting room.

Surprisingly soon, we boarded our next train. "This train will take us all the way to New York City. We ought to get there around 3:30 tomorrow afternoon," Mother told us.

Night came, and we tried to sleep, sitting up in the coach. Since we had only six seats, Mother held one of the younger children on her lap. Mother did not sleep well; her thoughts were with Dad. How she wished he were traveling with the family, sharing in making decisions, giving a helping hand. And how she longed for his loving touch. As she listened to the train's clickety-clack, clickety-clack, Mother reminded herself that every turn of the wheels was bringing her closer to her beloved.

Right on schedule Tuesday afternoon, the train pulled into Grand Central Station in New York City. Missionary V. Eugene Johnson was there to help with our luggage and hail a taxi to take us to the Lutheran Women's Home.

At the Home, Mother greeted the other Augustana Synod missionaries who would travel on the *Zamzam*. V. Eugene Johnson, his wife, Edythe, and their sons Vic and David, had previously served in Tanganyika, as had the Norbergs—Dr. Einar and Ida and their children, Marie, Carl, and Ruth. Another veteran missionary was Pastor Ralph Hult. Ralph had said goodbye to his wife, Gertrude, and their ten children in Missouri; like Dad, Ralph had volunteered to help out during the wartime crisis. Velura Kinnan and Esther Olson were two single women teachers on their first trip to Tanganyika. Including our family, this Augustana group bound for Africa amounted to nineteen. Tomorrow morning we would be boarding the *Zamzam*.

This evening, joined by other residents of the Home and by local pastors and friends, we shared in worship together; each missionary gave a brief greeting. When it was Mother's turn, she rose shyly. Her dark eyes meekly surveyed the group. Then she spoke, her voice strong with conviction: "I have often wondered how Christians can look forward so much to the 'last journey.' But now, as I have so much joy in going across the sea to be with my earthly bridegroom who has said, 'Come, all is now ready,' I can more easily understand the Christian's joy in responding to the Heavenly Bridegroom. When He invites us to the eternal feast, may we be ready and eager."

Mother sat down quietly and excused herself right after the service, explaining, "The children are ready for sleep." We headed upstairs to our assigned rooms.

The little ones were barely asleep when a friendly knock announced visitors. "Lillian, it's us." Mother recognized the cheery voice of Aunt Marie. From Chicago, Mother had sent a telegram to Dad's family in Meriden, Connecticut. Now Mother opened the door and lovingly welcomed Dad's mother, his three brothers, and two sisters-in-law.

Aunt Marie looked at Wilfred, who was fast asleep already. "Oh, he looks so much like his grandpa," she said, referring to Dad's father, who had recently passed away. "May we awaken little Wilfred, Lillian?"

"Of course." The precious time together was spent chatting, cuddling, and comforting. All too soon, it was time for goodbyes. Grandma Danielson gave Mother an extra long hug. "I am praying for you and the children every day, Lillian. I love you, and here's an extra kiss for Elmer," she said through tears.

"Grandma misses Daddy just like we do," Luella commented as Mother tucked the little ones in bed again. Mother lay awake a few more minutes. She could hardly believe all that had happened these past few days. 'Thank you, dear Father. Thank you,' her heart repeated. Then she fell asleep, our last night on land before riding the seas.

SIX
Farewell to America

The breakfast bell sounded early the next morning. The rest of the *Zamzam* group had nearly finished eating when our family, looking around self-consciously, appeared in the dining room. Ida hurried over with a warm hug. "We're so glad you're going on the *Zamzam*, Lillian. We've been praying for you." Mother smiled appreciatively.

As we children hungrily spooned into bowls of crisp corn flakes, Esther and Velura suggested to Mother: "When you are ready, let us take the three older children with us on the subway, Lillian. Mrs. Evald's daughter will take you and the little ones in her car." Mother was quite relieved, for she had wondered just how she would manage all six children and the luggage on the subway. God was helping us, step by step.

By mid-morning, Mother and the younger trio arrived at the pier in Hoboken. There was the *Zamzam*, secured by heavy ropes and gently bobbing in the quiet water of the harbor. The *Zamzam* was an old ship, Mother could tell, but she gazed on it as a trusted friend, a welcome vessel about to carry her to her beloved in far-away Africa.

As she walked toward the *Zamzam*, Mother sensed an unusual mood filling the air, for, despite the chilly March wind, the pier was lined with men, women, and children singing hymns as they bade farewell to friends and loved ones. It was a deeply moving scene.

Nodding appreciatively toward the singers, Mother walked up the gangplank, carrying Lois in her left arm and a couple of bags in her right. Luella and Wilfred clutched her coat. Laurence, Evelyn, and I were already waiting on deck, smiling broadly. "At last we're here! I can hardly believe it!" Laurence exclaimed.

A steward soon led the way to the two cabins assigned to our family. "Oh, these are wonderful," Mother commented. She liked the layout: the two cabins faced each other, connected by a narrow corridor, which served only our cabins. The corridor door opened onto the port side deck, on the main level. Mother realized we had a choice arrangement. In fact, she felt a bit guilty about being so fortunate, knowing that most passengers had cabins below deck.

Each of our two cabins had one single bunk and one two-level bunk. Of course, all three of us older children wanted the two upper bunks! Taking charge, Mother decided that Laurence would have the upper bunk in the cabin on the left. That cabin would be shared with Wilfred and herself, on the lower bunks, and Lois would sleep in the folding baby buggy. "Eleanor and Evelyn, you'll have to take turns with the upper bunk in the other cabin. Luella will have the single bunk." And so the matter was settled.

With hardly an inch to spare, the cabins were small but sufficient. We hung our clothes in the small wardrobe closets. Laurence put his precious stamp album on the shelf at the head of his bunk. Under one bunk, Mother placed the suitcase with underwear for the youngest children, plus their socks and quick changes of dresses and playsuits. It felt good to get somewhat settled again. These cabins would be home for the next six to seven weeks. "Kiddies, we won't need to move our things until we get off the ship in Mombasa. And then Daddy will be there to help us."

Wilfred grinned from ear to ear. He was still hanging onto his little red cap. He was going to wear it when he saw his Daddy again.

"Mama, when will the boat get going?" I asked impatiently in the mid-afternoon. Many asked that question, and nobody had the answer. All the rest of that day, the *Zamzam* moored idly at the Hoboken pier without an obvious reason for waiting; no more passengers or cargo were being added. The lack of explanation by the ship's officers made the situation even more puzzling and harder to bear.

The delay continued throughout the following day as well. 'And to think how we rushed to get here in time,' Mother thought again and again. Finally, at around 9:30 that second evening, March 20th, Mother passed the chief purser on deck. He waved a handful of official-looking papers, announcing, "Now we can sail!"

Sure enough, engines started humming, and anchors were raised. We could feel the ship vibrating, moving ever so slowly. Then something extraordinary happened: passengers gathered on deck and began to sing hymns. It started with only a few voices, and then, as more voices joined in, it became a mighty choir soaring with harmony and power. One hymn after another filled the air: "Lead, Kindly Light," "He Leadeth Me," "What a Friend We Have in Jesus," "Leaning on the Everlasting Arms," "Great Is Thy Faithfulness," and many more.

Mother listened from inside the cabin, as she now sat beside Evelyn, tenderly holding her hand. Evelyn had developed a sore throat and fever, even a chest rumble. The younger children were asleep already.

I had been among those out on the deck, listening and watching as the Zamzam glided out to sea. I was so impressed by the Statue of Liberty—it was a sight Mother ought to see. So I rushed into the cabin excitedly, begging, "Mama, please come see the Statue of Liberty! It is so pretty. You must see it, really!"

Evelyn murmured sweetly, "You go, Mama. I'll be OK."

Walking beside me, Mother stepped out on the deck and saw that most spectacular sight—the grand lady with the lighted crown and scepter, holding aloft a glowing torch, bidding travelers their last farewell as they left America's shores. Mother stood at the railing, taking in the beauty and meaning of it all: 'God bless you, America, 'til we return,' she sighed.

Standing there a while longer, listening to the inspiring

hymns still filling the air and watching the majestic statue re-
cede into the distance, Mother silently reflected on all that
had happened in less than three weeks. Even one week ago,
she had not known whether or not we would be on the
Zamzam. Now we were sailing toward the wide-open ocean,
on our way to Africa. 'Thank you, Father. We pray for a safe
journey. Bless and keep Elmer...'

Tears welled in Mother's eyes as she pictured her beloved,
alone at the mission house at Wembere, busy with his work
but waiting, waiting in loneliness. How she longed to be held
in his arms. Mother brushed aside a tear but, as usual, kept
her personal feelings to herself.

Then we returned to our cabins. Before long, we were
sound asleep, rocked by the gentle waves of the Atlantic
Ocean.

SEVEN
Life on the Zamzam

The *Zamzam* steamed steadily toward the deep ocean; the voyage had begun. Mother felt with certainty that our family's voyage on the *Zamzam* was God's doing—not hers, not Dr. Swanson's. 'God must have some special purpose for us,' she thought, as she thanked Him again and again for His help and goodness.

For Mother, traveling with so many missionaries was a special gift from God. This was quite unusual. With more missionaries boarding the *Zamzam* at Baltimore, the missionary count had grown to nearly three-fourths of the total of 201 passengers, which included 35 children. Bound for many different countries of Africa, the missionaries represented 20 Protestant denominations besides 17 Roman Catholic priests and teaching brothers. Another large group was the 24 drivers of the British-American Ambulance Corps, needed for humanitarian service in North Africa. Six tobacco buyers from North Carolina made up another contingent. The remaining passengers were traveling for urgent personal and business purposes. In wartime, no one traveled for pleasure only.

Indeed, the *Zamzam* was not a cruise ship. Some described it as "old and rickety." However, Mother felt she had never traveled on a smoother-riding vessel. The *Zamzam's* 8,300 tons plied through the waters proudly, under the watchful eye of Captain William Smith, a native of Great Britain. The *Zamzam* itself had British origins. She was built in 1910, given the name H. M. S. *Leicestershire* and had done service both as a passenger liner and as a World War I troop ship before she was sold to Egypt in 1933.

Under her new name, *Zamzam*, in honor of the sacred well near Mecca, she had next served as a transport ship for Muslims making their pilgrimages to Mecca. Even now, most of the crew consisted of Egyptian Muslims. They considered the ship holy, like her namesake. "Holy or not, this ship needs better care. It's filthy! It's a disgrace to any religion. I've seen dozens of cockroaches," one woman said in utter disgust. Others complained about the food; the generous use of spices reflected the culinary tastes of Egypt.

Mother did not have much time to think about how well the crew cleaned the decks or how palatable the meals were. She had her hands full, watching six children. She kept an especially close watch on her three younger children, spending hours and hours strolling up and down the deck, pushing the folding baby buggy. Usually the younger trio was delighted to have a ride together, even though it was a tight squeeze. Luella sat there, radiant with sweet smiles, her arms wrapped around Lois, sometimes leaning forward to give her little sister a kiss. Wilfred, at the other end of the carriage, would wear his red cap and smile broadly, for he was on his way to his Daddy. Little Lois sat in the middle, beaming with an impish smile, obviously happy to be the center of so much love and attention. Even though Mother sometimes felt like she was walking all the way to Africa, she enjoyed these carriage strolls. She knew her little ones were secure then, away from the open railing and the ocean's deadly depths.

The carriage rides also kept her little ones from disturbing others; Mother knew that not everyone appreciated children's noise and activities. As time went on, Mother found a mutual friend in Katherine Brill. The two of them sat together on deck, visiting as mothers do, while watching their little ones. One day they discovered not only that Wilfred and Edith had been born on exactly the same day, but that Mother and Katherine also shared May 6th as their birthday, Mother being a few years older.

Mother noticed that Pastor Hult often stopped by to talk

with us children. "Yes, I miss my Gertrude and the children. Do you mind if I spend some time with yours?" Pastor Hult's offer was beneficial to all of us. We children enjoyed his attention; he was kind and gentle, and he knew how to relate to children. Furthermore, his time with us gave Mother a few minutes for personal needs or for attending the women's devotional hour. She needed that relief from her constant vigil over her little ones.

Mother's concern for Laurence was a different matter, though. From the time he had learned to crawl, Laurence had been known for his adventurous spirit. Now, with Bobby, Vic, and Carl as cohorts, Laurence seemed to thrive on risk-taking. "Sonny, please don't climb on those frames near the railings," Mother begged. "And that open space up front, where there are no railings—you know, where you play hide-and-seek—that's only for the crew. You must stay away from there."

The captain himself warned the boys. "Anyone near the edge could get flipped overboard when the ship hits a big wave." Then, shaking his head for emphasis and staring right at Laurence, Captain Smith added sternly, "And I don't think we could rescue you, young chap. You'd soon be in Davey Jones' locker."

I posed another kind of challenge for Mother. Sensitive by nature and given to worrying, I had developed a terrible fear that the *Zamzam* was sinking.

Nearly every evening I would approach Mother in tears, "Mama, please come look. I know the boat is lower tonight. It's sinking. I know it is."

Mother would accompany me back to the railing. "Dear, I cannot see that we are riding any lower tonight," she would try to reassure me, as we both looked down at the churning, dark water.

"Mama, I know we are lower. We are going down." Mother did not realize that I simply did not comprehend how such a big and heavy ship could float. Furthermore, I had overheard dockworkers in Baltimore say as they put cargo in the ship's hold, "If we load any more on this ship, she will go down for sure." The words "go down for sure" still rang in my ears.

Unable to alleviate my fears, Mother would finally say, "We just have to trust God. He is with us."

Sometimes I would counter, "Mama, I know God is with us, but that doesn't mean He is going to keep the boat from sinking. Remember the Bible stories when bad things happened to God's people?"

"Yes, God does allow bad things to happen, even to His followers. But He is with us always, and He'll help us should anything go wrong," Mother would respond. "Besides, dear," she added, "we cannot do a thing about how high or low the boat rides in the water. Let's just leave the matter in God's hands and trust Him." She would give me a hug, and we would walk back to the rest of the family. But I kept on worrying.

Steadily and slowly, the *Zamzam* plowed through the ocean waters, going southward. Life among the missionaries began to take on a daily rhythm. Some adults engaged in language study; others gathered for Bible study groups. Most attended daily devotions. Mother did not have time for the study groups, but she tried to attend the devotional hour. It gave her much strength.

Schooling was organized for us children in a lounge, and soon books, pencils, and papers emerged, along with sixteen school-age children. Esther Olson and Velura Kinnan, who were on their way to Tanganyika to establish a school for children of missionaries, were our teachers.

"I'm really glad we have school," Laurence told Mother one evening. "It gives us something to do. And Miss Olson doesn't make me write the spelling words over and over." Mother smiled as Laurence continued, "You know what I like best? I like geography." Then he pulled a hand-drawn map from his pocket. "We learned about Trinidad today. Do you know that the *Zamzam* is going to stop there soon? Here it is.

Trinidad." He pointed on his map. "It's off the coast of Venezuela."

Just as Laurence had said, the *Zamzam* did make a daylong stop in the harbor off the coast of Trinidad on March 30th. Many passengers went ashore, but our family remained on the ship. Merchants came in little boats to the side of the *Zamzam*, hawking trinkets. The day went quickly.

After leaving Trinidad, the *Zamzam* headed toward Recife, Brazil, a port near the most eastern point of South America. It would take another week to reach Recife. Travel at sea seemed slow, very slow, but Mother rejoiced in each day, in each hour, and even each minute that brought her closer to her beloved Elmer and the mission work.

EIGHT
Blackout

"What in the world is happening?" Passengers were noticeably upset as the crew, with paint buckets and well-worn brushes in hand, stroked thick black paint across lounge windows, hall windows, and cabin windows, completely covering the glass surfaces. "And look, they are putting black tins over the porthole windows," Laurence observed. It was obvious that the *Zamzam* would be traveling blacked out.

"But that is not right," many were saying. "If we travel blacked out, it means we are trying to hide. We were told this is a neutral ship. 'Neutrals' have no enemies, so why should we hide?"

"I'm going to talk to the captain," V. Eugene announced. "We need to know what's going on here."

Passengers stood around tensely, awaiting V. Eugene's return. "I'm sorry, folks," V. Eugene began, "but it is bad news. Captain Smith says he has orders to travel blacked out, and that's all he will say. He refuses to say who gave the orders or why. I just couldn't get it out of him."

"What about navigation lights?"

"No lights. Period. Not even navigation lights. In addition, you gents and ladies who smoke, you'll have to use your matches and lighters inside. Even a tiny flicker could give us away."

"May I use a flashlight to get back to my cabin?" someone asked foolishly.

"No. No flashlights," V. Eugene replied firmly. "We'll have to turn off the corridor and hall lights before opening doors, too. This is going to take cooperation, folks, but we're in this together."

It was hard to digest all the changes at once. And why? Why was this happening? Mother sensed possible danger. She could feel tension in her body as questions flooded her mind: 'Is the *Zamzam* being pulled into the war? Will the blackout affect our getting to Tanganyika? Are my precious children going to be safe from danger? Heavenly Father, You know what is happening. Protect and keep us, according to Your will. Be with Elmer, too.'

At dinner, Captain Smith made an appearance. He seemed uneasy. His eyes darted about the dining room, not really focusing on anyone or any place. Brusquely, he announced that the *Zamzam* would be traveling in complete blackout from now on. Just as V. Eugene had reported earlier, Captain Smith would not divulge a thing about the source of this drastic order or the reason for it. However, he was stern and definite as he repeated instructions: "No lighters, no flashlights, not even a cigarette on deck. And whoever opens doors to the decks must be sure the light gets turned off first. Do you understand?" It was more of a command than a question.

Getting back to our cabin area, we drilled: knock first, wait to hear "light's out," then open the door.

Laurence had another concern. "Mama, you'll have to be careful going to the bathroom in the middle of the night. Don't trip or stub your toes on the deck chairs."

"And don't get lost and come back to a wrong cabin," I added.

Mother had to smile about our admonitions; it felt good to have her children looking after her for a change. "I'll be careful, kiddies. Everything will work out OK," she assured us in her usual, positive way.

The first night during which we traveled blacked out was very dark. The next morning, the sun was welcomed with new appreciation; we savored its glowing light filling the ship's cluttered deck and sparkling on the ocean's gentle waves.

As one might expect, the blackout became the major topic of conversation at the breakfast tables. Expressions of feeling betrayed were repeated often: "We were told before booking passage that the *Zamzam* was a safe and neutral ship and that it would stay away from war zones." Others reassured solemnly that God was in control and perhaps there was a greater need now to trust Him. Still others talked about practical matters, such as what to take with them if evacuation became necessary. The dangers of war had become real and immediate.

That day in school, we children found it hard to concentrate on anything academic. Imaginations ran wild, and heroic plans were made in the event the *Zamzam* was attacked. What about the chocolate bars in the commissary? They must not be lost. The older boys worked out a plan for rescuing all the candy; we girls smiled with approval and even a hint of admiration.

Night after night, the *Zamzam* now steamed along in total darkness. We learned to adjust. As Mother returned from the bathroom at night, she counted how many cabin doors she passed before reaching ours. Although she tried to avoid deck chairs, she sometimes bumped them, bruising her ankles and shins. One night, when Mother held out her arms to feel her way in the dark, she all but embraced a man coming in her direction. They both laughed heartily.

Then there was the night the moon lighted the deck and Mother happily commented to Mrs. Guilding, "Isn't it wonderful to be able to see in the moonlight, so we won't stub our toes?"

Mrs. Guilding chided gently, "Thank God for the blackest nights. Then we are safest."

Mother pondered yet one more insight of this unusual journey: God can use for good even what we might consider a bad situation.

NINE
Next Stop: Capetown

"It's been a good day, hasn't it, kiddies?" Mother commented as we wearily dressed for sleep, back on board the *Zamzam*. We had spent much of the day in Recife, a busy port in Brazil. Even the raindrops had not spoiled our delight in being on land again.

"It felt funny not to have the land moving," Evelyn observed. Having been on the rocking ocean for nearly three weeks now, the absolute stillness of ground had indeed seemed strange. Mother had especially appreciated the hours in the park. The quiet softness of grass under foot was a refreshing change from walking on the hard boards of a deck. Now and then, Mother had bent over to examine the exquisite beauty of a flower or to inhale its delicate fragrance. Most of all, she enjoyed watching us children romp and play as if we had no cares, no worries, no restraints. How adaptable children are, Mother realized.

Using the baby buggy for the little ones, we walked to a shopping area. Bags of coffee beans lined the sidewalks, spreading the aroma of coffee everywhere. Inside one shop, Mother had found small toys and knickknacks at a reasonable price. Even though it meant she went without lunch, Mother figured she had enough spending money to delight each of us with at least one small purchase.

Now back in our cabins on the *Zamzam*, Laurence was busy examining the addition to his prized stamp collection. "Thanks, Mama, for the new stamps," he said sincerely. "And I really like my new helmet, too. Thank you." To buy a tropical helmet for Laurence was the main reason we had gone ashore in Recife. Laurence was prone to sunstroke, and, as the *Zamzam* was now traveling under the direct sun's rays in the equatorial zone, Mother was concerned about Laurence's health. Besides, he would need a helmet in Tanganyika.

As Laurence modeled his new safari helmet again at bedtime, Mother was struck by the resemblance between her young son and her brother Gust. Thoughts of her loved ones in Kansas brought her a wave of homesickness as she crawled into bed for the night.

As happened often, Mother's thoughts shifted to Tanganyika. She yearned to be with Elmer again. Mother could picture her sweetheart waiting on the dock at Mombasa as the *Zamzam* would be guided into the harbor and secured firmly. Then the gangplank would be lowered, and Elmer would board the ship. He would walk straight toward her. Their eyes would meet, brimming with love, and he would put his arms around her and hold her close. Tears filled her eyes just thinking of their reunion. But here she was, on the *Zamzam* in a port in Brazil, still a month from reaching Tanganyika, thousands of miles away.

'Forgive me for being impatient, heavenly Father. Thank you for bringing us this far,' Mother began, as she talked with her Lord before falling asleep.

The next day, April 9th, the *Zamzam* headed out to sea again, beginning a diagonal, southeasterly course across the South Atlantic. For the next eleven or twelve days, we would plow through endless water without any sight of land. Our next scheduled stop was Capetown, South Africa.

Most passengers would disembark in Capetown. Others, including our Augustana group, would remain on board to continue the journey. No doubt, new passengers would join the *Zamzam* in Capetown, and cargo would be exchanged. From Capetown the *Zamzam* would be routed along the entire east coast of Africa, bound for Alexandria, Egypt, her home port.

In Recife only two new passengers had boarded the ship: Charles Murphy, an editor of *Fortune* magazine, and Dave Scherman, a photographer with *Life* Magazine. Mr. Murphy looked the part of a distinguished gentleman: middle-aged, tall, and handsome, with a gentle air of authority. Scherman, on the other hand, was young, in his early twenties; he exuded boyish charm and winsome kindness. Their congeniality made them welcomed by the rest of the passengers.

TEN
Scares at Sea

A couple of nights after leaving Recife, near midnight, Mother awakened to repeated blasts from the ship's horn. 'Something's wrong,' she realized. She opened the door to the deck and stepped out. Oooohhh. She stood ankle deep in cool water. All she could see in the darkness was water, water everywhere. 'Are we sinking? Is the ship down this far?' she wondered.

Mother hurried back into the cabins, awakening us as she pulled out the life jackets from under the bunks. Hastily tying a jacket on Wilfred, then one on Luella, she urged us older children, "Tie them tightly, kiddies..."

Suddenly someone was knocking at the door. "Mrs. Danielson, Mrs. Danielson." It was Pastor Guilding. "I am pulling your door shut tighter. Some light is leaking out."

"But what is happening?" Mother asked anxiously.

"Oh, we've just had a sudden downpour, and I guess the drain got plugged somehow, so the deck is flooded. That little rim along the edge is holding the water. That's all."

"But the horn?"

"That's just the fog horn. It's pretty soupy out tonight. We wouldn't want to risk a collision," Pastor Guilding explained, adding reassuringly, "It's too foggy for any enemy action, anyhow. There's nothing to worry about."

Greatly relieved, Mother turned to us. "Everything is OK, kiddies. It's just the foghorn. Take off your jackets and get back to bed."

"Mama, let's thank Jesus the *Zamzam* is not sinking tonight. I thought it was really happening," I said, my voice tense with fear. Mother led in prayer, then gave us each a goodnight kiss again. How good it felt to snuggle in our bunks and go back to sleep! Soon Mother could hear the deep breathing of her slumbering children, unmindful of the dull horn blasts which still cut through the heavy night fog.

Talk at the breakfast hour the next morning was unusually lively. All around the dining room, passengers were asking each other, "Did you hear the fog horn last night?" "Were you worried?" "What did you do?" A few had slept right through it. Some had figured it out right away. But the most common answer was "Yes, at first it worried me, too."

Then someone would add: "Did you hear about the Danielsons? Lillian got the children out of bed and had them put on their life jackets—they were about to leave for their lifeboat!"

Mother felt rather embarrassed about the episode, but she had simply done what seemed wise at the time. After all, she had six precious lives in her care, and it was better to take precaution and be prepared than to regret it later. She also reasoned, it had served as a realistic drill, compared to the haphazard lifeboat drill held one bright afternoon under an officer's command. At that drill, our life jackets had not even been taken out from under the bunks.

Furthermore, last night's incident had made Mother aware that our family had a total of only six life jackets. Since Lois used the baby buggy as her bed, a seventh jacket had not been added to the cabins' normal quota of one per bed.

Soon after breakfast Mother announced, "Kiddies, I am going to talk with the purser about another life jacket. Sonny, please keep Wilfred and Luella here in the cabin until I get back." Then, picking up Lois, Mother left. I tagged along.

Mother found the purser in his office. He smiled kindly. "Good day, Mrs. Danielson. How may I help you?"

"I have no life jacket for my little one," Mother explained, nodding toward the squirming child in her arms.

"Oh, I see. She is yet so small. A life jacket would not do her any good—she would drown anyway."

The purser did not mean to be unkind, but his words cut through Mother's heart like a knife. 'My baby drowning? No! Something must be done!'

"Please, I must have another jacket," Mother persisted. "I am entitled to seven jackets, and we have only six. Surely you have another jacket someplace. Please look."

Sensing Mother's determination, the purser excused himself and, after a few minutes, returned with an old jacket, adult-size and full of holes. "I'm sorry, but this is the best I can do, Mrs. Danielson," the purser offered apologetically.

Thanking the purser, Mother took the dilapidated jacket and returned to her cabin. Then she took out a needle and thread and began sewing. Not only the newly acquired jacket but also the other jackets were in dreadful disrepair. Mother stitched deftly, mending holes, replacing tie strings, reattaching and shortening straps.

I stood nearby, watching, wondering, and worrying. Finally, I spoke my thoughts. "Mama, if you are so sure the *Zamzam* will not sink, why are you fixing the life jackets?"

Mother answered carefully. "God wants us to take care of ourselves and do all we possibly can to keep safe and well. Beyond that, we leave it in His hands." Mother put the jackets back under the bunks, hoping she would never need to touch them again.

Easter Day came on April 13th, filled with joyful celebrations of Jesus' resurrection. First, there was a children's service in the lounge, attended by adults as well as by children. Pastor Hult proclaimed the Easter message triumphantly, along with recitations and songs by us school-age children. "Christ the Lord is ris'n today! Alleluia."

Even the pre-schoolers took part. Luella held little Wilfred's hand, singing with faith and trust, "Yes, Jesus loves me."

Many times during that service, especially when her children were reciting or singing, Mother's eyes filled with tears. 'Heavenly Father, thank you for these precious jewels. Keep them singing Your praises always.'

A "breaking of bread" worship followed the children's service. Holy Communion always held deep meaning for Mother, but partaking in Communion this Easter morning gave her an unusual sense of being renewed and strengthened in her inner being.

In the early evening, there was a service of praise held out in the open on the starboard deck. With the surging waves still visible in the twilight's glow, this service spoke with great assurance that Christ has won the final victory, no matter how the billows of life buffet us. That was a powerful message for travelers at sea.

The special glow of Easter still filled Mother's heart the next day. She did not even feel anxious when, around 3:30 in the afternoon, at teatime, the *Zamzam* started to make a wide turn. Eventually, the *Zamzam* was heading due west, back toward South America. Passengers gathered on deck, scanning the vast ocean in all directions, looking for some reason for the sudden change of course. No other ship was in sight. The weather, too, raised no problem.

"What's going on?" some passengers wondered aloud, obviously perturbed. They looked toward the officers' deck and saw Captain Smith peering through his binoculars, studying the eastern horizon. A crew member was stationed in the highest lookout post on the mast; he, too, seemed to be focusing toward the east.

Hour after hour passed, the *Zamzam* steaming full-speed toward the west, as if fleeing. The officers kept to themselves, not even joining the passengers after dinner. Their air of secrecy fanned greater uneasiness and even anger. "We have a right to know what is happening," many complained. By now Mother, too, felt concern.

As she tried to sleep that night, she could feel the added vibrations of the ship's engines, straining with increased speed.

The next morning, we could tell by the position of the sun that the *Zamzam* was back on its correct course. There was a notice from Captain Smith on the bulletin board: "Re change

of course yesterday: precautionary measure due to alert re
suspicious vessel in area. No further cause for alarm."

The day went smoothly.

The next day, April 16th, everything seemed normal as well.
"The captain must be right, there is no reason for alarm,"
many observed as they were thinking of the next stop, Capetown.

ELEVEN
"Kiddies, Be Brave"

April 17th, 1941, Mother awakened earlier than usual and lay in her bunk musing, 'Only four or five more days and we'll be in Capetown...The longest part of the trip will be over...Best of all, a letter from Elmer will be waiting there...'

Suddenly, without warning, Mother's peaceful reverie was shattered by a loud, explosive rumble. 'A clap of thunder,' she told herself. But no, it was not the same as a Kansas thunderstorm. She had better check.

Quickly and quietly, Mother stepped out onto the deck and peered into the early morning. The sun had not yet risen. Both the sky and the water were a dull blue-gray color. Suddenly, a red spurt of fire pierced the morning mist, accompanied by another loud rumble as a shell barreled toward the *Zamzam*. There, three to four miles distant, Mother saw a dark, sinister-looking warship crouching on the water. This was enemy action.

Keeping her wits about her, Mother hurried back into our cabin area and announced as calmly as she could, "Kiddies, we're being fired at by an enemy boat. Get dressed and put your life jackets on. Help one another. Be brave in Jesus."

Mother began to pull life jackets out from under the bunks. She tensed as she heard another shell being fired. There was a dull splashing sound as that shell fell short of its goal. But what about the next one? The shells were coming steadily now, one about every ten seconds.

Quickly replacing her nightgown with an everyday dress, Mother saw Laurence pulling his best shirt and Sunday suit over his pajamas. Across the corridor, Evelyn and I put on our best dresses, leaving on the pajama bottoms. Quickly we tied on life jackets. Then, grabbing Luella by the hand, we hurried to Mother's cabin.

The next shell hit below waterline. The cabin shuddered, and the ship began tilting noticeably. Little Luella started crying softly. Laurence looked pale. "Jesus loves you, kiddies. Never forget that—no matter what happens," Mother assured us.

'Hurry! Never mind dressing the little ones,' Mother told herself, as she pulled life jackets over pajamas and tied straps. The younger children had no understanding about what was happening. All they wanted to do was to take off those bumpy jackets and get back to sleep. They whimpered and fussed, tugging at the straps. No sooner was one jacket tied than another jacket was removed.

If ever Mother wished Dad was there beside her, it was this morning. 'I must not despair. The children need me,' Mother knew. Another shell whined overhead. "Kiddies, Jesus loves you," Mother repeated.

It was hard to stand now, with the cabin floor tilting toward the deck door. What if the *Zamzam* rolled over, trapping us inside? "Sonny, maybe we should leave now while we can," Mother wondered aloud.

"I don't know, Mama. Maybe we are just as safe staying here," Laurence answered, wise beyond his years. 'Sonny's right,' Mother thought. 'Where is one safe on a ship under fire? If we are seen on deck, we might become an easy target. And it does seem that the tilting is not getting any worse.' So we stayed. Mother bent over to tie Wilfred's and Lois' jackets again.

Another shell whizzed overhead. It made a whining noise. Mother felt someone clinging to her skirt. It was little Luella, trying so hard to be brave as big tears trickled down her cheeks.

The next shell hit a lower corridor with horrific, sundering sounds, followed by sharp screams. Someone had been hurt badly, we knew. The air was soon filled with the acrid smell of explosives; the moans and cries from the wounded were pitiful and sobering. Mother stood there solemnly, waiting, listening. There was no signal from the ship's whistle. What should we do? We children huddled around Mother. She was our tower of strength. Even the little ones had quieted by now.

The shelling kept on and on, now almost ten minutes. The seconds between shells seemed like an eternity, as we wondered where each new shell would hit. Picturing the worst, Mother felt a lump in her throat. Would she lose any of her precious children? Would they be left without a mother? She tried not to think about what could happen. Instead, she reassured us, "Kiddies, whatever happens, remember that Jesus loves you even more than Mother and Daddy do. He is with you, always. Never forget that."

The words were barely out of her mouth when a shell hit the room directly above us. A steel girder crashed to the floor up there, shaking our cabin so violently that our lavatory cracked and was left hanging on its pipes. Pitchers and tumblers on the glass shelves shattered, and even the mirror was splintered, showering our tiny cabin with slivers of glass. The lights waned. The little ones started crying again. The polluted air became difficult to breathe. The next shell could hit our cabin. Indeed, Mother thought, the gate to heaven seemed wide open; death seemed so near. From the depths of her soul, Mother begged silently, 'Father, save us for Elmer's sake. Thy will be done. If we are to live, I need Your strength, Heavenly Father. Help me, help me.'

"Did you hear that?" Laurence asked. "Someone said we should throw ourselves flat on the floor and be ready for the next one. But, there's broken glass all over the floor. What shall we do?"

Suddenly, in rushed the ship's purser, his hair disheveled, blood trickling down his cheek below his broken glasses. "Mrs. Danielson, can you manage?"

"Yes, but I haven't known what to do. I've heard no signal."

"The whistle was damaged by one of the first shells. The

shelling has stopped now. Get to your lifeboat station as quickly as you can." Then he was off, to look after someone else.

Mother bent down to tie the strap on Wilfred's jacket one more time. Then, spreading her arms around us as best as she could, she prayed aloud, "Heavenly Father, may we all be together again in heaven if not in this world, and take special care of Daddy in whatever he has to go through."

Picking up Lois and grabbing Wilfred by the hand, with Luella clinging to her dear Mama's skirt and we three older children scurrying alongside, Mother led us to our assigned lifeboat station: number eight. It took only a minute to reach the station, a few yards to the left of our cabin, on the port side.

Our lifeboat, which had already been lowered from the upper deck, was hanging there alongside our railing. Assisted by one of the ambulance drivers, we scrambled over the railing and found places to sit in the swaying wooden boat, as it dangled about twenty feet above the ocean. I tried not to look down at the deep, dark water below us. Pastor Hult was nearby in our boat; he reached out with a comforting touch.

Just as Mother was about to climb in, she realized she had left her purse in the cabin; her purse contained the passports. "Oh, kiddies, I must go back to the cabin. I'll be right back," she announced, turning to leave.

"No, Mama. No! No! Stay with us. Please!" Our frantic cries were too much. Mother stayed. 'Never mind the passports,' she thought. 'Maybe we'll need no passport except to the heavenly shore, and Jesus has already granted that.'

Once Mother was seated in the lifeboat, Lois was handed to her. Seconds later the crew began to lower the lifeboat. Mother realized that, without a doubt, she would have been left behind if she had gone back for her purse. She shuddered at the thought. It felt extra good to have baby Lois' chubby arm wrapped around hers.

Our boat descended jerkily, as the rope unwound from an overhead pole. When we were nearly at the water, the rope suddenly slipped off the pole, and, from high above, the heavy wooden pole came hurtling down toward us. Mother bent over to protect Lois. Ouch! Ooooh! Mother got a terrific blow on her crown, hard enough it could have knocked her unconscious or even injured her fatally. Before long, she had a swollen lump.

But Mother had no time to think about the pain. The lifeboat touched water with a big splash. Carrying a full load of about thirty passengers, the boat soon steadied itself. Quickly, the crew grabbed the oars and started rowing feverishly, heading toward the wide-open ocean to the rear of the *Zamzam*. The crew members were in an absolute panic. As some rowed, others threw their arms heavenward, crying to Allah, voices frenzied with fear. Having considered the *Zamzam* to be holy, they had believed nothing bad could ever happen to their ship. What was happening was unfathomable to them.

Glancing around at the other lifeboats, it seemed that most passengers were coping without hysteria, even though some had to jump into lifeboats from rope ladders. Others were stranded on rope ladders or were still on the *Zamzam*'s deck because several lifeboats had pulled away only half full. Mother saw some passengers swimming to their lifeboats. She was so thankful to be in a lifeboat, not in the water.

But oh! something was not right. The little toe on her left foot, apparently cut by broken glass, began to smart. Looking down, Mother saw more than an inch of salty ocean water sloshing about her shoes. 'It is probably from the splash when the boat touched down,' she tried to reassure herself.

Then someone shouted with alarm, "Our boat is leaking! It's like a sieve—look at these holes! Help! Help!"

"Quick, start bailing!" someone else yelled, grabbing an empty tin can. Only one other can could be found.

Mother glanced around. Her eyes rested on Laurence, wearing his new helmet. "Use my son's helmet," Mother offered. Reluctantly Laurence took off his prized helmet and gave it to waiting hands. With swift, rapid strokes, the helmet was filled and emptied, over and over, over and over. Others scooped with cupped hands. Even we children tried to help. But the water was coming in faster than it could be thrown out. Shrapnel had left dozens of small holes. Within minutes, the lifeboat was filled halfway up to our knees.

"Let's go back to the *Zamzam*. Stop rowing! Go back! Go back!" one of the men shouted, gesturing toward the *Zamzam*. The crew understood the message, but they did not heed it. Instead, they kept on rowing and rowing, senselessly taking us farther and farther away from the *Zamzam*. The lifeboat moved more and more slowly as it filled with water, sinking inch by inch. The water was up to our waists now.

The boat couldn't take much more, Mother knew; we would be going down soon. Her heart of mother love was nearly breaking as she clasped Lois more tightly, clutched Wilfred's hand, called to Laurence to look out for Luella, and smiled encouragement to Evelyn and me. Her precious, precious children. Would she see us all again?

"Kiddies, be brave in Jesus," she called out.

TWELVE
In the Deep Ocean

With a sudden lurch, the lifeboat went down, pulling us with it. Mother was fully under water. The salty water smarted her eyes, and she squeezed them shut tightly. Mother had the presence of mind to keep a tight grip on Lois, but she lost her hold on Wilfred. Instinctively, Mother kicked with her feet. She bumped someone else's legs. Then, foof! She and her baby bobbed to the surface.

Shaking water off her face, Mother saw that Lois' jacket had come off and was blocking her baby's face. Quickly, Mother pushed the jacket to the side. Lois smiled in relief and clutched her little arms around Mother's neck, too young to be concerned that now she wore no life jacket. All that mattered was that she was with her Mama.

And there, nearby, was Wilfred, sputtering frantically, his head tilted back so far that the ocean billows were splashing over his little face. Gripping Lois more tightly in her left arm, Mother reached for Wilfred with her right hand. She grabbed the back of his life jacket and pulled him upright. But whenever Mother let loose, Wilfred's head would tilt back again with his face awash from the waves. Mother realized Wilfred needed constant help.

But where were her other children? Looking around, Mother could see Evelyn and me a few feet away, and, not far from us, Laurence. But where was Luella? A fearful thought seized Mother's heart. She looked around again. No Luella. Luella was slight of build. Had she dropped out of her life jacket? Mother's heart cried out in anguish.

Then she saw Laurence burst into action. As if he desperately needed to clear a space, Laurence was shoving and pushing and then kicking a burly crew member. Finally able to maneuver at that particular spot, Laurence reached down, grabbed Luella's arm, and yanked her to the surface. She had been trapped under water. Luella gasped and then held her breath for several seconds before she got the rhythm of breathing again. She looked terribly frightened. But she was alive!

Although she looked calm, Mother was aware of the dangers facing us as we now bobbed in the ocean. Swallowing too much salty ocean water could make us gravely ill, so Mother called out, "Kiddies, keep your mouths shut. Shut tight. And pray."

The ocean was quite smooth that morning, but even the slight waves and swells could carry us far apart. "Eleanor, grab Evelyn. Hold onto each other and come in closer," Mother cautioned.

Although the water felt cool in the early morning, we were in the tropical South Atlantic. Mother dared not think of what might be lurking beneath the surface. She knew there was the possibility of sharks, and they would be attracted by the fresh cut on her foot.

Looking at Wilfred beside her, Mother now realized that he was wearing the smallest life jacket, the one intended for Lois. If Wilfred, who was only three years old, had worn his own jacket, he would very likely have dropped out and drowned by now. God was helping us by even using our mistakes.

Mother looked around again. Since we were the only children in the water, it was quite easy to spot us—Laurence, Evelyn, myself. But where was Luella? Mother could not see Luella! Fear stabbed her heart again. Had Luella gone down? 'No, Father, no!' Mother cried silently. Then, in the next moment, as a billow lifted an adult to the side, Luella was in view again, her tiny head poking out of her life jacket, bobbing helplessly in the waves like a rag doll. She looked even more frightened and bewildered. It tore Mother's heart, but she could do nothing about it; she had no more arms with which to help or hold her little ones. But she could speak comfort. "Remember, kiddies, Jesus loves you. He is with us." Mother's sincerity and faith seemed to encourage others also. No one asked her to be quiet.

An oar was floating nearby. Pastor Hult grabbed it and pushed it under Mother's arm, giving support as she held Lois. Eventually the wooden lifeboat surfaced again, now bottom side up. Ali, one of the crew members, quickly scrambled aboard and called to Allah.

"Here, help these little children," Pastor Hult admonished. Reluctantly, Ali bent over and pulled Wilfred, then Luella aboard the overturned lifeboat. Mother felt relief to see two of her little ones out of the water. How small and helpless they looked against the backdrop of the vast ocean. They were cold, too, especially Luella. With her teeth chattering and her knees bent upward, Luella sat there rocking herself back and forth, trying to warm herself. That sight Mother would never forget.

Evelyn, too, was pulled from the water eventually to join Luella and Wilfred. Laurence and I stayed in the water, sometimes hanging onto the edge of the lifeboat. Mother was nearby. From time to time, she felt Lois squirm restlessly. Mother held her baby more firmly, lest little Lois slip to the ocean's grave.

Though Mother was greatly relieved that all six of us children were alive, she was also fearful. How long could these old jackets keep us afloat? What would happen in the next hour, the next day? Would she ever see her beloved Elmer again? Mother tried not to imagine the anguish Dad would feel when he learned what had happened. He was very tenderhearted and sensitive. How would he handle the news?

In the midst of these anxieties, Mother never forgot God's personal and real presence. Over and over she sang in her heart: "Hiding in Thee, Hiding in Thee, Thou blest Rock of Ages, I'm hiding in Thee." She knew only God was sustaining her and giving her courage. We children needed that strength, too, so she called again, "Remember, Jesus loves us; He is with us."

Only forty-five minutes had passed since our lifeboat had capsized, but the wait for help seemed much longer. Like ours, one or two other boats had also sunk into the water; passengers wearing life jackets dotted the billows and floated helplessly in the deep ocean. Other lifeboats idled, filled to capacity, still above the surface. Badly crippled but still afloat, we saw the tilted *Zamzam* nearby. It was a solemn, dismal scene.

"Look! The warship is coming toward us," someone near us cried out. "They have machine guns. I suppose they will now finish us off."

The warship bore a swastika flag. Someone else said, "I would rather die than become a Nazi prisoner."

Mother hoped we children had not heard these comments. She was not concerned about the emblem of the ship; she just hoped for help before someone drowned.

All of a sudden, joyful cheers arose: "A rainbow! Look! See the rainbow!"

We looked up and there it was—a complete rainbow, each color brilliant and distinct. It arched breathtakingly above the crippled *Zamzam*, as if it had been painted right there, above us helpless survivors, above the approaching warship. No artist could have better depicted God's hope and triumph in the midst of destruction and despair.

It was a holy moment.

THIRTEEN
Rescued by the Raider

The warship steamed closer and closer. We could feel vibrations in the water. Then all was quiet. The warship cut its engines. A motorboat was quickly lowered onto the water. Help was on the way!

But no! The rescue boat veered toward the other group in the water. Mother's heart sank. 'How much longer can we stay afloat? Will they come back for us? Father, help us, help us.'

Help came soon, as a second motorboat was launched, headed straight toward us, and stopped. The strong arms of German sailors reached down to take baby Lois from Mother. Then Mother was pulled from the water and helped into the swaying motorboat. Lois scrambled back into the comfort of Mother's arms.

Almost numb with cold and relief, Mother watched as each of us children was helped into the motorboat. She longed to hug us, to touch us, but the little boat was crowded and rocking. She could only smile at us.

Our motorboat began chugging toward the waiting warship, a raider, an armed ship in disguise operating against merchant shipping. It bore the name *TAMESIS*. German officers and sailors lined the upper deck, quietly surveying the scene of helpless men, women, and children approaching their ship. It had become apparent by now that the machine guns had been readied for use on sharks, not humans.

As our motorboat pulled alongside the raider, a rope ladder was released, swaying clumsily from the top deck all the way to the water far below. Laurence, Evelyn, Luella, and I were among the first to climb. The wall of the ship went straight up, more than three stories high, and it scared us. A German sailor climbed right behind each of us, in case we faltered.

At the top, Germans met us kindly. One who could speak English said to Laurence, "We didn't want to do it, my boy, but it was orders."

When it was Mother's turn to climb, she hesitated. Her legs seemed like rubber. And what would happen to Wilfred and Lois?

Pastor Ohman, sitting nearby, sensed Mother's reluctance. Taking little Lois from Mother's arms and wrapping his coat around the shivering toddler, Mr. Ohman said firmly, "You go ahead, Mrs. Danielson. Your baby will be all right. Go now!"

Bravely taking a tight hold on the rope, Mother cautiously stepped from the idling motorboat onto the first rung and began the climb. We children were relieved when we saw Mother come over the railing and join us on the high deck. A solemn officer pulled off our soaking life jackets and threw them to the deck with a thud. "Come into a warm room," he invited kindly.

"Thank you, but I must wait for all my children."

Glancing at us four shivering children clustered around Mother, the officer uttered in astonishment: "Eins, zwei, drei, vier. Mein Gott! Are there more?"

Just then a voice called from the motorboat, "Coming up now, Mrs. Danielson!" A large straw basket was hauled over the railing. Someone said, "There's a baby inside." Mother hastily pulled loose the cord closing the basket, and there sat Lois, her big brown eyes still bigger now. With "Mama" on her lips and her little arms outstretched, she soon snuggled in Mother's arms again. The officer, visibly moved, brushed aside a tear.

Soon, a second closed basket came over the railing. Mother knew Wilfred was inside. Sure enough! When he saw the rest of us standing there before him, he smiled a big wide grin from ear to ear, happy to be safe up high, safe out of the big,

big pond.

With all six of us children now aboard the raider, our family was ushered toward the officers' quarters. When we were almost there, a guard suddenly guided Laurence toward a different corridor. A look of fright crossed Laurence's face. Where was he being taken? And why? Would he ever see his family again? "We'll see you soon, Sonny," Mother called out, trying to reassure her anxious son.

Once inside the officers' cabins, the wet clothes were removed from us children. Our cold, naked bodies were rubbed briskly with towels. We were wrapped in dry towels, barely big enough to cover us older girls. Mother understood now why Laurence had been separated, he being older and needing privacy. Before long, he joined us, also clad in nothing but a skimpy towel. He seemed self-consciousness but greatly relieved to be back with the family.

We were dry, but still cold. We could not stop shivering. Little Luella looked slightly blue. A young, kind-looking officer standing nearby motioned toward the officers' bunks, indicating we should crawl under the covers. We did so gladly. The officer even helped lift Lois and Wilfred into bunks and gently tucked in covers, not satisfied until all six of us were warm and comfortable. Then the officer passed around chocolate cookies and we munched most appreciatively.

Now, seeing all her children snuggled safely in bunks, Mother fell on her knees and opened wide the floodgates of her soul. First, the tears came in trickles. Then, the trickles became quiet sobs. Mother's small body shook. We looked on in bewilderment. We had never seen Mother cry like this. The officer tapped Mother on her shoulder and offered a chair, not comprehending that she was now finding much needed comfort, communing with her Lord: 'Thank you, Father. Thank you. Without Your help, we would have been lost. Oh! To think that all the children are still alive. All of them. Thank you, Father, thank you. Please care for my sweetheart. He will worry. Bring us together again, according to Your will. Thank you, Father...'

She prayed and wept until it seemed she had no more tears.

After about an hour of resting and being warmed in the officers' quarters, we were told to follow a guard. Mother picked up Lois, and we began the descent down three flights of metal stairs, way down to the bowels of the ship. Finally, we reached a very large room, where others from our lifeboat had already gathered. On opposite long sides, there were rows of wooden bunks, three high. The adjoining smaller room also had bunks, and that is where the guard suggested our family choose beds.

Seeing the black-and-white checked slipcovers on the slim mattresses, Mother had an idea. "May my son use one of the mattress covers to wrap around himself?" she asked. The guard nodded with understanding. Before long, Laurence was grinning sheepishly in his strange, new attire, but at least he was fully covered.

Mother, herself, was still wearing her wet dress, which was now getting stiff from the drying salt water. Her long dark hair, which was normally pulled back in an attractive bun, hung loosely, disheveled. Her hairpins had been lost in the water, and she had no brush or comb. But that was not important now.

Laurence seemed sick to his stomach, no doubt from the nervous strain. He lay down.

Evelyn voiced another need. "Mama! I need to use the toilet. I can't wait much longer."

"Me, too," echoed Luella. Mother went ahead toward the bathroom area. Uh-oh, one of the toilets was clogged, and the floor was covered with more than an inch of filthy water. Not wanting her children to walk in that stinky, dirty mess, Mother picked up the younger children, one by one, and carried them to and from the toilets. She even lifted Evelyn through the worst area.

Mother had another bother: the pain in her left foot grew worse, and it throbbed relentlessly. Mother removed her shoe. Ouch! She winced as blood spurted from a deep gash in the flesh near the little toe. She realized she must have cut her foot on the broken glass in our cabin.

Mrs. Ohman was sitting nearby. "Lillian, I have some Mercurochrome and a bandage. Let me help you," she offered. Gently she treated the wound and then wrapped a towel around the swollen foot, for Mother's shoe no longer fit.

While Mother attended to us children and her injured foot, more and more passengers and crew from the *Zamzam* came aboard the raider, one motorboat load at a time. They gathered in that large room in the bottom of the ship. Rumors circulated about this friend or that one who might have died or drowned. We felt grief. But then we would see that person walk into the room, alive and well! 'This is what resurrection morn will be like,' Mother thought.

Not everyone was there, however. "Little Elaine Morrill is still missing. The crew would not wait for her when her family was getting into their lifeboat. She was left on the *Zamzam*," someone reported. Elaine was the same age as Luella. Mother could imagine the parents' anxiety; she breathed a prayer for them.

There was a spirit of caring and sharing. Seeing us Danielson girls clad only in towels, one friend gave us a sweater and two pairs of panties. Someone else had a little dress for Luella. Another friend gave us safety pins to help fashion the towels into garments. Others had nothing to share except a hug and a prayer.

We had not thought about eating until we saw the guards setting up temporary tables. Then came tin bowls, which the guards partially filled with stew. It was thick, made of rice and vegetables. Mother encouraged us to eat, but we seemed to have lost our appetites. Even the bread did not appeal to us. Nor did the limeade. "Try to drink at least a little of it," Mother suggested, mindful of the danger of dehydration. We tried, but we did not swallow much of anything.

The meal finished, a guard announced that everyone should assemble on the forward deck. Glad to leave the stuffiness and sickly odors of the lower room, Mother picked up Lois and led us up the metal staircase. Reaching the deck, we blinked as our eyes adjusted to the bright tropical sun. There, to the right, was the *Zamzam*, tilted even more. Pumps kept the ship afloat. The *Zamzam*, now silent, wounded, and dying, revealed a sorry, sad sight.

We watched the raider's two motorboats, laden with mounds of blankets, trunks, and boxes, as it made one trip after another between the raider and the *Zamzam*. It was obvious the Germans were salvaging what they could from the ill-fated *Zamzam*.

"Look, Mama! There's my bicycle!" Laurence suddenly exclaimed. Sure enough! It was the blue and white Schwinn Dad had purchased in Salina for Laurence's tenth birthday last June. Others spotted prized possessions, too. "I hope they bring my doll," Evelyn said wistfully. Mother smiled, thinking about what a loving little mama Evelyn was for her dolls. Mother wondered if her sewing machine and Dad's violin were being saved. And she surely hoped some of our clothes were being transferred to the raider.

"My cap, my little red cap," Wilfred was saying. With his little red cap, he planned to go to his Daddy.

FOURTEEN
God's Saving Hand

There was a stir toward the front deck. It was shortly after noon on April 17th. Someone was making an announcement. "Be ready to step forward for registration, Lillian," V. Eugene advised kindly as he walked by.

Like a roll call, names of survivors were being compared with the passenger list retrieved from the *Zamzam*. It was good to learn that little Elaine was now safe with her family aboard the raider.

Before long, Mother heard her name called. Shyly she stepped forward. "Mrs. Lillian Danielson, traveling with six children," an aide announced loudly, emphasizing the number six. A towering officer looked down at our meek, little mother and asked compassionately, "Mother, how many of your children survived?" It was an awesome moment. Looking squarely into the officer's eyes, Mother answered humbly, loud and clear, "I thank God He saved us all."

Roll call was finally completed. But the officer was not yet satisfied. He whispered to his aide, and the two of them checked the records again, as if looking for an error. Finally, the officer was ready to speak. "We have never had an experience like this," he began. "No one is missing. Not one life was lost today. Three men are very badly injured, but they are alive at this time. There are other injuries less serious. It is most unusual that nobody was drowned or killed by the shells." He paused. "We fired fifty-five shells, but only nine hit your ship. Unbelievable. Unbelievable," he said as if to himself, shaking his head.

Then, clearing his throat and regaining military composure,

the officer continued, "Because no life was lost, we do not have to report this incident until we want to, and I do not think the captain intends to report it. We apologize for what has happened, but we surmised that your ship was aiding the Allies. You must remember, you were traveling blacked out," he added emphatically. He paused and then continued, "Ja, this is wartime, and this is a ship of war. The British are looking for us. It is not good to keep civilians on a warship. We will transfer you to another ship as soon as possible."

"How soon might that be?" V. Eugene asked boldly.

"I don't know. Maybe tomorrow. Maybe the next day," the officer responded cautiously. "But now, we must finish sinking the *Zamzam* and be on our way. We have been in one spot too long already. If you wish, you may watch. We have put three time bombs on the *Zamzam*. They are about to go off."

There was quite a bit of moving about as passengers positioned themselves to watch the *Zamzam*'s sad ending. Dave Scherman, the photographer, and V. Eugene Johnson had been given permission to use their cameras. Around them, at the warship's railing, other passengers waited solemnly.

Mother knew it was best that we children not see the sinking, so she took us to the opposite side of the raider's deck. Laurence, however, begged to watch, so Mother allowed him to join his buddies at the railing.

A funereal silence permeated the atmosphere. Then we heard it—a loud, reverberating boom, as if something had exploded deep inside the *Zamzam*. Two more similar, resounding thuds followed. Nobody spoke.

Soon Laurence rejoined us, obviously shaken. "The bow went under first," he reported tensely. "Another blast was in the back, and it tipped the *Zamzam* nearly on its side, the port side. Even the funnel broke off. It went so quickly. I can hardly believe it."

We walked slowly toward the railing, where we had seen the *Zamzam* minutes earlier. Now we looked at the empty ocean in disbelief. The *Zamzam* was gone. Completely gone. All that was left was churning, bubbly water and bits of debris. Machine guns were blasting the debris so that no trace would be left to guide the raider's enemies. Mother felt downhearted. Our "home" and most of our earthly goods were gone. Our plan for getting to Dad was shattered. Loss and emptiness flooded her with grief.

Then she felt the warmth of Lois in her arms and the tug of Luella at her skirt. And there was Laurence gently holding Wilfred's hand, and Evelyn and I also stood nearby—all of us whole and healthy. Looking at the six of us, Mother's sorrow suddenly turned to praise: 'Thank you, Father. Thank you. Whatever we lost is nothing compared to the riches Elmer and I have in our children.' The only ache she felt now was for Dad.

"Oooh! My toe hurts more and more," Mother sighed as she hobbled back down the metal stairs to the ship's lower level. Pastor Hult noticed Mother's limp and advised firmly, "You better see the doctor, Lillian."

Mother agreed, and, within the hour, she faced a stern looking German surgeon in the warship's small hospital unit. A few minutes later, Mother was returning to us children, her toe stinging from a generous application of iodine. A German guard, seeing Mother's freshly bandaged foot without a shoe, hurried from sight and soon returned with a felt slipper. It was much too big, but it gave protection. God was at work, caring for us even through our captors, Mother realized.

Finally, it was bedtime. After prayers and kisses, Mother stretched out on her bunk, eager for a night of rest. She lay still, trying to stifle the itchiness caused by residue from the ocean's salty water. The salt was on her skin, in her matted hair, in her stiff dress.

We children were restless, too. The salt was irritating our skin, the surroundings were strange, and most of all, the trauma of the sinking and the rescue was troubling our thoughts. "Kiddies, try to relax and get to sleep," Mother urged. Then she started to hum softly, as she prayed silently: 'Father, let the terrible experience we had today not scar the children. Please don't let them have bad memories and fears. Help them to forgive the enemy and to look for good in whatever happens.' Mother kept humming and praying until she could hear us breathing calmly and regularly, sound asleep.

Sleep, however, did not come easily to Mother. Her nerves were on edge, and she reacted to even the slightest noise. She tried not to think of the morning's trauma, but flashbacks haunted her: the shelling ... getting to the lifeboat ... its harsh descent, and the terrible blow to her head ... the water filling the lifeboat ... being submerged in water ... keeping a grip on little Lois ... the fear of Luella's drowning ... the approaching warship ... climbing the rope ladder ... Over and over, the scenes appeared in her mind.

She kept thinking of her sweetheart, too. 'Father, give Elmer hope. Keep him strong. Bring us together again, according to Your will, Father...'

Mother was finally drifting off to sleep after eleven o'clock, when the raider's alarm bells began clanging loudly. Startled, she sat up. Then she began to count seven short clangs and one long clang. That signaled danger!

Trying not to show fear, Mother awakened us and hustled us out into the large room. Other *Zamzam* survivors huddled there, too, sitting on bunks, standing sleepily, wondering what the alarm meant. Something important definitely was happening, for the German sailors could be heard rushing up the stairway.

The room's only exit leading directly to the deck was up those metal stairs, and that exit was closed securely by a locked iron door. "We're trapped!" someone blurted with panic.

A German guard peered in cautiously through a small window in the locked door. In return, V. Eugene Johnson pounded on the door, and shouting in German, demanded an explanation. "We have sighted another ship," the guard responded in his mother tongue, with V. Eugene interpreting. "We do not know yet if it is an enemy ship or the freighter we summoned for you."

"What will happen if it is an enemy ship? We're helpless, locked down here like this. We don't even have life jackets," V. Eugene protested.

"You'll get jackets up on deck," the guard answered. That was little comfort, knowing it would take time to untangle the heaps of jackets, many of which were soaked. Moreover, how long would it take for all of us in this room—about two hundred—to get to the deck using that one set of narrow stairs? If it was an enemy ship approaching, we only had a small chance of survival.

V. Eugene called again, "How soon before we can know what ship it is?"

"About ten minutes," came the reply.

Those ten minutes seemed like an eternity. Many passengers were praying quietly; some were weeping. Mother stood there with Lois sleeping in her arms and the rest of us clinging to her quietly. She felt so weak and helpless; she knew she could not endure another shelling and sinking tonight. Like a child begging a favor from a parent, Mother prayed silently, over and over, 'Dear Father, please keep us from danger. Please spare us. Please, Father.'

Suddenly, the German guard opened the door and commanded loudly, "Go back to bed! Tomorrow you will be transferred to the ship that is arriving now. It is the freighter we had summoned." Mother had never heard more welcome words. She was filled with thankfulness. God had again spared us from death.

As we lay down on our bunks again, Mother suggested, "Kiddies, we lost our Bible today, but I am sure you know some Bible verses to share. Will each of you older children quote a verse before we go back to sleep again?"

Without hesitation little Luella started: "Jesus Christ, the same yesterday, today, and forever." Evelyn followed with "The Lord is my Shepherd; I shall not want." I quoted "In nothing be anxious; God careth for you." Laurence's choice especially touched Mother: "O why are ye fearful, O ye of little faith?" Mother felt so blessed by her children's faith and trust, and by our willingness to share it. She treasured this moment.

Then we heard Pastor and Mrs. Steele praying nearby. After praying for their teenage son and daughter and other loved ones in the States, the Steeles continued, "Lord, bless the little children on board tonight, especially the Danielson children. Help all of us to adopt them as our responsibility." It was comforting to know that other passengers were praying for our family and were willing to help. God was at work in many ways, through many people, encouraging and renewing Mother with strength and hope for whatever lay ahead.

Indeed, the journey was not over.

As Mother awakened the next morning in the dreary, lower level of the raider, she felt an inexpressible joy in simply being alive. Life is a precious gift, not to be taken for granted, she reflected.

A couple of hours later, all *Zamzam* survivors were allowed out on deck. As we emerged into the bright, clear sunshine, we saw to the right a freighter bobbing lazily, connected to the raider by long, heavy ropes. The freighter was about equal in length but not as high as the raider. We could see the name *DRESDEN* on the freighter. It was to be our new home. Motorboats were already transferring luggage and supplies from the raider to the *Dresden*.

We children were full of questions: "Mama, how soon will we get on this other boat?" "Where are the cabins?" "When can we get some clothes?" "Mama, where will the *Dresden* take us?" Mother had no answers. She, too, had questions and anxieties.

Mother felt a glimmer of hope, however, when she learned that the raider's captain had arranged for a meeting with five of our men, representative of the various passenger groups. V. Eugene Johnson was appointed the spokesman for the Protestant missionaries. "Please ask if there is any way to let Elmer know we are all right," Mother requested. "And how soon will we be able to go to Tanganyika?" The men were gone almost an hour.

Finally, V. Eugene reappeared on deck. "Sorry, Lillian," V. Eugene began, "but Captain Rogge says there is no way you may contact Elmer. In fact, just as the officer said yesterday, the captain does not plan to report the sinking." V. Eugene paused and added somberly, "We'll just have to pray for our loved ones as they wonder what has happened to us." He was thinking especially of his two teenage children in the States.

By now, many *Zamzam* passengers had gathered around V. Eugene. He continued, "I was favorably impressed by the captain. He had been a full captain in the German navy. His name is Rogge, Captain Bernhard Rogge. We can be thankful we are in the hands of such a decent man, folks. He apologized for what happened, but he pointed out we were traveling in blackout. Captain Rogge said he remembered having seen the *Zamzam* years ago, when she was an English troop ship during World War I. He did not know the *Zamzam* had been sold to Egypt."

"But why didn't he stop firing sooner? Didn't the *Zamzam* signal our identity?" someone asked.

"You know, that brings up a miraculous chain of events. Here's what happened: when the shelling began, the *Zamzam*'s radioman had hurried to send out the SOS distress call to nearby ships. However, before the radioman could send the message, a piece of shrapnel had grazed him, causing him to fall, slightly injured. Then another officer had rushed to send the SOS, but, as he was about to touch the machine, the next shell destroyed the radio antenna. Therefore, no message was sent, not even a blurb of one letter. Captain Rogge said that, had any message gone out, for his own safety, he would have torpedoed the *Zamzam* and not stayed around to pick up survivors. We were that close to death."

"Surely God was with us. That timing was more than an ordinary coincidence," commented a passenger.

"So you see why the shelling kept on as long as it did. Even the wire on the Morse blinker had been damaged. Finally

Captain Smith found a flashlight and signaled our identity. Then the firing did stop immediately. Captain Rogge says he was stunned to see all of us civilians, especially women and children. I believe his apology is sincere."

"But why is he treating us Americans like prisoners? We're not at war!" someone protested angrily.

"Officially, we are 'guests' here, but, for all practical purposes, we are 'prisoners.' I don't think the Germans know what to do with us yet, except to transfer us to this other ship."

The discussion went on, but Mother did not stay; the children were getting restless. As she walked away, she could hear V. Eugene saying that evidence had been found in Captain Smith's cabin supporting the assumption that the *Zamzam* was sailing under orders of the British Admiralty. Who really was to blame for what had happened? The answer was not clear. But Mother knew for certain: war is evil and innocent people suffer.

FIFTEEN
Aboard the Prison Ship

It was afternoon before the transfer took place. All *Zamzam* survivors were moved from the raider to the freighter, except the three severely injured men still in need of care at the raider's hospital unit. A few women and men needed assistance, but at least they could leave the warship. Mother realized again how fortunate our family was. Except for her cut toe and the bump on her head, we had no injuries.

As a whole, the transfer went smoothly. A gangplank descended from the raider to the motorboats. As Mother climbed into the motorboat, her oversized slipper fell into the water. Quick as a wink, an Egyptian crew member swooped the slipper from the water and, with a big smile, gallantly put the slipper back on Mother's bandaged foot. Mother smiled in return.

Minutes later, we were walking up another gangplank, boarding the *Dresden*.

The *Dresden*, a freighter with accommodations for thirty-five passengers, now faced the monumental challenge of providing space and provisions for the three hundred thirty-some *Zamzam* survivors, including passengers and crew.

The men were directed toward the cargo holds. Single women and other women traveling without children were assigned to the lounges, while mothers and children were given the few cabins.

Upon learning that there were two single beds in each cabin, Mother immediately suggested, "Our family can manage with only one bed. Someone else may have the second bed in our cabin." Mother's offer was very sincere, but perhaps a bit naive. A long, awkward silence followed. Who would want to share a small cabin with six young children?

Finally, Mrs. Powell spoke up graciously, "I come from a family with eight children. I will be happy to be with the Danielsons." She was about ten years older than Mother and had only one child, a daughter who had been left behind in the States. However, these two missionary mothers shared a deep common bond: their husbands were awaiting them in Africa. Mrs. Powell became our roommate. Being gentle and quiet, she had the good sense to wait to come to bed after we children were asleep. Then she tiptoed cautiously, careful not to step on those of us who were sleeping on the floor.

Usually Mother began the night lying down between Lois and Wilfred on our family's one, narrow bed. Before long, Luella would be speaking softly in Mother's ear, "I miss you, Mama," and somehow Luella would snuggle her way next to Mother. As soon as the three little ones were asleep, Mother would move quietly to the floor, joining us older children.

Only a thin pad was between the hard floor and us. Life jackets served as pillows. We had no sheets; each of us was given one blanket. We were crowded, sleeping closely together, usually side by side. Sometimes, when the ship rocked in strong waves, we would awaken in the morning to find ourselves bunched together at one edge of the cabin. Other mothers and children were also crammed eight or nine in a small cabin normally accommodating two persons. And yet, our situation was better than that of the women in the lounges. They had even less space and no privacy at all.

For the men it was even more difficult. The Egyptian crew was assigned to one cargo hold, and the male passengers and *Zamzam* officers were put in the other hold. More than a hundred men were crammed together in the stuffy 54 by 54-foot cargo hatch. They slept on lumpy thin pads, made from old sacks filled with cotton. The pads were placed on loose planks that covered the steel floor. A rope ladder was the only means for entering or leaving the hatch. When it rained, as it often did in the tropics, the hatch had to be kept closed, making the lack of ventilation almost unbearable.

During sunny, daylight hours, the men were assigned to the lower deck in the fore part of the ship, separated from the women and children. The men stood in long lines for meals, eaten picnic-style, using enamel bowls, tin cups and spoons. Chores and calisthenics became part of the daily routine. The German guards carefully watched the men at all times. Mother heard that some of the young men were very restless and angry about the whole situation. She prayed often that the spirit of the wiser and calmer men would prevail. The captain of the *Dresden* had not been very cordial when he first met the men. "I'm Captain Jaeger, captain of dis ship. If you fellows do as you're told, den everyting vill be alright. But if you don't, vell, ve vill take care of dat, too." With those brusque words, he had stomped off.

Almost from the start, the *Dresden* became known as "the prison ship." That title fit our situation. Warily, we arrived in the dining room for supper that first day. Long, wooden planks had replaced the usual tables. In order to seat so many women and children, we had to eat in shifts. Finding seven places together, we bowed our heads and prayed our table prayer, hopeful for satisfying food.

Before long, a guard appeared with a big cooking pot. Reaching for the stack of tin bowls, he doled out a bowl of watery soup for each of us. Was this our meal, we wondered? We could see only a few pieces of potatoes and a few small peas and a string or two of beef floating in the tasteless broth. We were quite disappointed. Mother felt sorry for us. "Here, kiddies. You eat my vegetables and meat," she offered, as she fished out the solids from her soup and shared with each of us equally.

"How about some bread," she suggested.

"But Mama, I can see bugs baked in the bread!" we protested.

"It won't hurt you, kiddies. Go ahead—close your eyes and try it," she begged. But none of us ate the bread that evening. We were not yet hungry enough.

Mother hoped breakfast would be more appealing. Instead of soup, however, only a thin, bland gruel made of flour and water was doled out. Some called it "glop." There was no milk or sugar. "Mama, do I have to eat this? It tastes like wallpaper paste," I complained. The others agreed with me.

Mother looked around helplessly. There was nothing else to eat. "Kiddies, just try it," she urged kindly. Inwardly she felt pity for us; she hoped we would not be subjected to this kind of food for very many days. For now, however, we needed nourishment, so she encouraged cheerfully, "Let's see who can empty the bowl first!" But even our normally competitive spirits did not motivate us to eat. We left the table with empty stomachs.

By noon that day, we actually welcomed the watery soup, and Laurence took a few bites of the dark bread, trying not to think of the bugs he could see baked into it. That became the pattern: gruel for breakfast, soup for lunch, soup for supper. Sometimes the soup had a few pieces of macaroni instead of potatoes. By the third day, most of us began to eat the gruel. Soon, we were eating the bread too. Even when we saw worms in the soup, we ate it. Real hunger left no room for being finicky or stubborn.

We had to make many adjustments those first days. "Hang onto your bowls," Mother warned. A sudden lurch of the ship could mean a meal was lost, as bowls often tipped and clattered to the floor. We older children cooperated well. With Lois it was another story. She was at that "me do it" stage—"Little Miss Independence"—insisting on handling her spoon and managing her bowl all by herself, then wailing when it spilled.

"Oh, if only there was some milk for Lois," Mother mentioned to Ida. "And I don't know what to do for Luella." Most of us Danielson children were of sturdy build, but not Luella. Having not eaten well while on the *Zamzam*, she was now becoming thin and gaunt. Mother could not coax Luella to eat, and what little food she consumed was often lost in vomiting.

"I can understand your concern, Lillian," Ida responded. "I wish Einar had some medications or supplements to help." There were several missionary doctors on the *Dresden*, including Einar, Ida's husband, but none had any supplies. The lone bottle of cod liver oil someone had salvaged had been shared and finished already.

Mother's heart ached when we begged not only for food, but also for water, especially when we were traveling under the hot tropical sun. The ship's supply of fresh water was limited and therefore carefully rationed, doled out in the mornings and evenings. If only we could keep some of the water to wet our faces or tongues in the warm afternoons. Where could the water be stored? The only place to leave it was in the cabin's lavatory. Try as she would to keep on eye on three-year-old Wilfred, somehow he would find the water, splash and play in it, then pull the plug, fascinated and delighted as he watched the gurgling water spin down the drain.

Having no toothbrushes, toothpaste, or soap, we did the best we could with personal hygiene, usually using salt water. We did not even have a comb or hairbrush until a friend purposely broke her long comb and gave us part of it. The only way to get rid of our terrible tangles was to cut off some of our hair, even Mother's lovely, long, dark hair.

Our cabin had no toilet, so we used the common toilet off the corridor. "Mama, I can't wait much longer," I complained one morning, trying hard to be a proper little lady as I stood in line. More than fifteen women were in line ahead of me. I fought back tears. I knew what was going to happen, and I could not help it. Evelyn, too, fidgeted and squirmed. Mother looked at us with sympathy; she felt our embarrassment and humiliation as puddles formed at our feet. Surely there was a tin can which could be kept in our cabin for such emergencies. Within a couple of days, Ida found a can for us. Mother marveled that something as ordinary as a tin can could be appreciated so much.

SIXTEEN
In Search of Clothing

Shortage of clothing was another concern aboard the prison ship. With Lois having diarrhea, the need for more underwear had become critical. Mother was still wearing the same dress she had worn in the ocean. By now it was absolutely filthy. Laurence was still draped in that mattress cover; the rest of us were garbed in makeshift combinations. Certainly some of our clothing had been salvaged. Mother wondered how soon we could get it.

On the third full day on the *Dresden*, it was finally announced that the head of each family would be given twenty minutes to search through the luggage taken from the *Zamzam*. Mother could hardly wait for her turn! Arriving at the baggage area, she found trunks and suitcases stacked helter-skelter. Several minutes passed before she recognized her brown army blanket, its corners tied together, bulging with clothing. Mother bent over to untie the blanket.

"No, lady. Step aside and wait," a guard ordered firmly. "There is clothing in there for others also. They must come." With her precious, allotted time fleeting, Mother tried to be patient. Finally someone else came, and the blanket was untied, revealing clothing belonging to several different families. Apparently, on the morning of the sinking, the blanket had been spread on the deck of the *Zamzam*, and clothing from various cabins had been dumped into it. Fortunately, Mother found dresses for us girls and for herself, and a couple of playsuits for Wilfred. But there was nothing for Laurence, absolutely nothing. Poor Sonny, still wearing that mattress cover.

Three days later, Mother was given another opportunity to search through luggage, this time for only fifteen minutes. She spotted her two small steel trunks. But alas! The trunks were locked, and the keys had been left in the cupboard on the *Zamzam*, now at the bottom of the ocean. The guards tried in vain to open the trunks. Happily, though, Mother found the little brown leather suitcase in which she had kept underwear and socks for the children. However, when the lid was opened, Mother discovered that the suitcase was completely empty; its contents could not be found anyplace. Troubled and discouraged, Mother had to leave her search that day empty-handed.

After another three long days, Mother had another turn to search in the baggage room. Now desperate for clothing, she went straight to the guards and asked them to use an iron bar to pry open her two locked trunks, even if it meant ruining the trunks. What a find! There were shoes for each one in the family except Laurence. Mother's plaid coat was there, too, plus more dresses, playsuits, and even a shirt for Laurence; but there were still no trousers or shorts for him.

By now most survivors had found some clothing. Those who had something to share were glad to help others. However, nothing was found for Laurence. Not only was he still draped in the mattress cover, but the skin of his bare feet started to crack. Mother began asking for help for her son.

The next day Captain Smith, former captain of the *Zamzam*, approached Mother. "Are you still looking for shoes for your son?"

"Yes, but so far I have not found anyone who can spare a pair," Mother replied.

Captain Smith held out a pair of white leather shoes. "I have this pair, size nine. A lady has been using them, but now she has found her own shoes. If your son can use my shoes, take them." Accepting the shoes, Mother thanked the captain graciously, overwhelmed that a person having had the rank of Captain would care about her son. The shoes were too big of course, but padding the toes took care of that problem.

Gratefully Laurence slipped his sore feet into his new shoes and self-consciously paraded out to join his buddies. Mother smiled proudly as she thought of her son "filling the captain's shoes."

Captain Jaeger, captain of the *Dresden*, had been observing the survivors' needs, too. Although he appeared to be curt and callous, some thought that his outward demeanor disguised a kind heart. One morning, Captain Jaeger called the women together. "Vimen, I vant you to make de best of dis situation. I vill do the best I can to land you some day, but I can make no promises. Dis is var days. Vimen should not travel mit so many kids. By the vay, vere is de voman mit de six kids?" Mother shook in her size twelve sailor's slipper as she stepped forward, expecting a stern reprimand. Although she tried to watch her children, she did not know what mischief one of them might have done.

Captain Jaeger blurted out, "Is it your boy vot is running around here mitout any pants on?" This made the women snicker in a friendly way, and even Captain Jaeger lightened up with a smile, putting Mother at ease as she told the story of why her son was garbed in the mattress cover.

"Vell, so you vant to make him some pants?"

"Yes, I'd like to, but I have nothing to work with."

Captain Jaeger said that two sewing machines had been salvaged from the *Zamzam* and were now available for use. Wonderful news! A few women had scissors and thread, but what could be used for cloth? "Here, Lillian, Walter says you may cut off the bottoms of his trousers," Marcella Ohman offered later that day. Another friend also gave trousers for cutting. Gratefully Mother stitched together some simple shorts for Laurence, made tight with a drawstring.

Laurence, too, was very, very thankful as he folded up the filthy mattress cover, donned his new shorts, and felt like a somewhat properly dressed young man again. Again, through various means, God had provided for our needs.

SEVENTEEN
Rendezvous with the Raider

"Mama, how long are we going to be on this boat? And where are we going? When will we see Daddy?" Evelyn was asking.

"I wish I could tell you, dear," Mother responded, lovingly putting her arms around her seven-year-old.

"Someone said we are just killing time, going in circles until we meet the raider again," Laurence said. He was right. Nine days after the *Zamzam* had been sunk, the *Dresden* prepared to meet the warship again, probably not far from the site of the sinking.

There was considerable excitement as the rendezvous drew near. Everyone wondered about the health of the three injured men who had been left on the raider: how are they doing? Moreover, has Captain Rogge announced the sinking by now? Do our loved ones know what has happened to us? Is there any way we can let them know we are alive?

In addition, several men from the *Zamzam* had drawn up a two-page letter of protest to be presented to Captain Rogge: "It is not only illegal but an act of inhumanity to keep us circling and running in the South Atlantic. Save for bread, the men have lived on liquid food for eight days."

About the women they had written, "The seventy-six women and thirty-five children are living under conditions that, if prolonged, are bound to affect their health. Five of the women are pregnant..." The letter demanded freedom soon, pointing out that the United States was not engaged in the war and that most of the passengers were citizens of the United States.

Letter in hand, a small delegation of men met with Captain Rogge, face to face, aboard the raider on April 26th. Charles Murphy, the editor from *Fortune*, served as spokesman for the *Zamzam* survivors.

When the delegation returned to the *Dresden*, many gathered to hear the report. We were saddened by the news that Ned Laughinghouse was near death. "Vicovari and Starling are improving, but they still need to be kept in the raider's hospital unit."

"Has the sinking been announced and what about our freedom?"

"Captain Rogge says he has not announced the sinking yet, and he says there is no way we may communicate with anyone. As for what will happen to us, he says Americans will be set off in some neutral place and given freedom," Mr. Murphy responded.

"Where might that be?" someone interrupted.

"He mentioned that Americans might be taken to South America or the Canary Islands, or perhaps even transferred to another ship at sea, but he refused to be specific. And he made no promises about that."

A sigh of disappointment could be heard. Mr. Murphy continued: "But Captain Rogge did promise some eggs, and he is sending over canned milk for the babies. In addition, men with families aboard will have visitation hours. However, that's about it. This is wartime, and we just have to endure, he says. I am sorry we could not bring you a better report."

Then we were all ordered inside our cabins, so no one could watch as the raider steamed away in secrecy.

The raider was gone; we returned to the deck. Mother's hopes of contacting Dad or rejoining him soon had been crushed. She felt her spirits sinking. As she stood on deck, looking out on the vast, vast South Atlantic, she felt so small, so alone. Tears began to fill her eyes. The strain of hardships and uncertainties was wearing on her. Tears began rolling down her cheeks. She knew she needed a good, hard cry.

Quickly asking Ida to watch Wilfred and Lois, Mother headed to our cabin. Alone, she let the tears come, and with the tears came a litany of woes: every day was such a trial, watching six children, trying to keep positive and hopeful for their sakes, feeling weak from lack of food, worrying about the children's health as she saw them losing weight, especially Luella. In some ways, life on the *Dresden* was harder than the day the *Zamzam* was sunk.

'And what is going to happen? Will we ever get on land and be set free? And how is Elmer? Oh, dear Father, I feel so broken and helpless. I thought we were doing Your will in going to Africa, and now it has come to this. Where will it end?' Mother wept and wept as she kept talking with God. Deep in her soul, Mother knew her Heavenly Father understood and accepted her cry.

Finally, after she had poured out her despair and fears, she deliberately began to think of God's goodness. She counted her blessings, which were many, even in these terrible circumstances. 'You have promised grace to meet every need. I need to trust you more, Father. Forgive me for doubting, for relying on myself,' Mother confessed. 'Fill me with your righteousness, your strength. Only then can I cope.' Eventually she could pray, 'Thank you for loving me so much you died for me. My suffering is nothing compared to yours, dear Jesus. Thank you, dear Lord.' Mother knelt beside her bed, listening, reflecting, feeling her Savior's strength and power.

Then, with a smile on her face and a song in her heart, she returned to her children.

EIGHTEEN
Coping and Caring

Several changes actually did come after the rendezvous with the raider. As promised, men with families on board were given visitation time for two hours every morning. Mother knew it must be heart wrenching for husbands and wives to say good-bye each day, realizing they might not meet again in this world. In dangers of war, nothing can be taken for granted, not even tomorrow.

Another change was the availability of condensed milk for children under two. After a few days, the age limit was raised, but Wilfred refused to drink the sweet, syrupy stuff. Luella, too, could not stomach it. Cookies from the commissary on the *Zamzam* were now turned over to mothers for distribution to the children only. One cookie each day after lunch—not before. What a treat! "I have never tasted anything so good!" Evelyn remarked, slowly licking the frosting in a sandwich cookie. Another occasional treat was jam on bread. Little things meant so much, Mother realized.

She wished she could give her children other treats, but she had nothing to give, except what she could provide abundantly—faith and love. Every morning we began the day with prayer, and every night we had devotions. After devotions, Mother would give us each a goodnight kiss. When she came to Luella, there would always be a second kiss for Mother, with Luella sweetly saying, "That one's from Daddy."

Mother marveled at how well we children were coping. For the most part, we seemed to be taking hardships in stride and behaving quite well. She told us that we made her proud.

There was one exception: our conduct at school. The setting might have been partly responsible for our misbehavior. Because space on the *Dresden* was so limited, all of us school children met as one class, squeezed together on the metal steps of the open stairway to the upper deck. Pencils, papers, and books had been lost in the sinking, which limited school to oral drills, such as spelling or math, along with devotions and singing.

Trouble was, we older girls were stricken with giggles, prompted by the boys' wisecracks. Once we started giggling, we could not stop—even during devotions. Our irreverence greatly concerned our teachers, especially Esther, who prayed aloud about our disrespect. However, her prayers made us girls giggle even more. And the more we giggled, the more Esther prayed.

"Eleanor and Evelyn, you need to control yourselves," Mother chided. "Miss Olson and Miss Kinnan are putting themselves out to have school. You are making it hard for them."

"I know, Mama. I don't mean to giggle, but I just can't help it," I answered. "The more I try not to giggle, the more it just happens."

Deep in her heart, Mother felt the matter was not all that serious. "I'd much rather have the girls giggling than crying or complaining," Mother told Ida. "But I will apologize to Esther and Velura, and I hope the children improve."

"Yes," Ida responded. "I feel a bit ashamed of my girls, too, but don't you think it is a reaction to the tension with which the children live? I think they are holding up beautifully, really." Mother agreed. And although we tried to control ourselves, our giggling continued.

One part of school-time that did go well was the singing. A gifted musician, Esther knew how to lead hymns and choruses, such as "Running Over...(My Cup Is Full and Running Over)," "For God So Loved the World," and "Safe Am I...(in the Hollow of His Hand)." We loved to sing, especially "Safe Am I." It gave us comfort and hope as we faced the uncertainties of life aboard the German prison ship.

Besides school, we children passed time in simple games. Hide-and-seek and jumping rope seemed to be the favorites. Checker boards and checkers, made of cardboard, served well when the weather was not windy. The men made Chinese checkers using wooden pegs for marbles. The boys took up woodcarving, and the girls begged their mothers for knitting needles and yarn. Story telling consumed many hours as well.

For the most part, harmony and good spirits characterized the adults too. Books were shared. Survivors talked and talked with each other. Devotional times were held. There was much hymn singing, usually accompanied by instruments. The missionary men had a small band—two trombones, an accordion, and a guitar—and sometimes Dave Scherman played the ocarina. At the women's evening devotions, Rhodie Olson accompanied with her violin. Mother loved to listen to the rich tones Rhodie produced, beautifully supporting and carrying the words of favorite hymns.

Much time was given to prayer. Besides praying for our own welfare, survivors prayed for families back home or in Africa. Many were praying for Dad and other special loved ones who must be wondering and worrying about the whereabouts of *Zamzam*ers. There was also prayer for home congregations and for mission work, across denominational lines. We had become one large family. It was a good feeling—a heavenly feeling.

Mother thought of all humans as family, even of our German captors. Perhaps they felt that way about us, too. They always treated us kindly, despite our being their prisoners, constantly guarded and closely observed.

One of the German guards was especially good to the children. Sometimes he appeared on deck with an orange or an apple, saved from his own meal. He would cut the fruit into small sections, and divide them carefully among twelve or more children. There was only a small piece for each, but Mother noticed how we relished it. She hoped that we would remember the kindness of the guard and not just the tasty fruit.

Another guard seemed fond of little Lois, often asking to hold her. He did not speak English, and Mother did not speak German, but she knew there must be a story behind his interest. One day, he carried a small photo of twin girls, Lois' age, and Mother understood that the twins were the guard's daughters, back home in Germany, born after he had left for sea.

"He probably doesn't like being here any more than we do," Laurence commented. Laurence's maturity and insights impressed Mother. We were growing up quickly through this experience.

On the other hand, Mother realized that we were still young children. We needed to talk about our childish fears, our regrets, and our hurts. We missed our Daddy and wondered each day what he was doing. We talked about playmates back in Kansas and things we missed. Evelyn and I wanted new dolls to replace the ones that had been sunk. Mother promised she would buy us dolls again some day.

"Mama, do you know what I want most of all?" Laurence asked one day.

"What is it, Sonny? Maybe I can get it for you," Mother suggested, supposing he might want a bat and ball or a bicycle. She hoped it would be nothing bigger, such as a motorbike.

"I want roast beef, mashed potatoes, and gravy," Laurence replied sincerely. Mother felt her eyes fill with tears.

The women also talked about what they missed. Things previously taken for granted were held in new appreciation. A bar of soap, for instance, was treasured. And, as the women now wore makeshift combinations of clothing, they often reminisced about their wardrobes of former days.

One evening, after hearing several women describe their losses, Mother felt inspired to put some thoughts on paper. She penned a poem, which she titled "Loss and Gain Reveries":

You say you had a loss of this and that pretty gown
When the South Atlantic you crossed and this item and that
went down.
How we might sit and count this gift and that we did treas-
ure;
Into the dollars they mount and some whose worth we can't
measure.
"But what shall we do without them, those gowns we had
made with care?
We had adjusted them neck to hem so they'd be ready to
wear."
"But friends, there is one robe I didn't lose that day!
It was given me long ago by Him who is the Truth, the Way.
It's not a tattle-tale gray as those washed by my feeble hands.
No—it's a pure dazzling white, washed in the blood of
God's Lamb.
My own dress is as filthy rags for I am so full of sin.
Jesus gives me a robe of righteousness that I may stand spot-
less in Him.
So why should I ever count my loss of these earthly things
which went down,
So long as my Jesus on the cross I didn't lose—nor my crown.
Friend, have you put on the robe Christ is waiting to give to
you?
You cannot stand before God's throne until His robe doth
cover you.
Dear Jesus, just cover me with this robe and Thy holy self,
That others may see Jesus only, my crucified, living in me."

NINETEEN
Running the British Blockade

One week had passed since the sinking, then two weeks, then three. Even without paying attention to the sun's position, Mother knew that the *Dresden* was steaming north, day after day, for the air became cooler and cooler. Some days had become actually cold. Most folks stayed inside as much as possible.

When it was necessary to be out on deck, we wore whatever we could just to be warm. Style was not important. Mother had cut our old brown army blanket in two, and made drawstring capes for Laurence and Evelyn. I was lucky. The Buyses had given me a raincoat. Mother wore the plaid coat that had been salvaged from the *Zamzam*. The coat's full cut provided shelter and warmth for the younger children, like chicks gathered under the wings of a mother hen. From scraps of yarn, Mother had knitted caps for all of us. Wilfred was especially pleased. "I go see Daddy," he said with a big grin, as he put on his new red cap.

"I wonder where we are going," Mother commented to Ida. "Didn't Captain Rogge promise to put us off at a neutral port or transfer us to a neutral ship at sea? I don't see anything like that happening. There's been plenty of time—we're into the second week of May now."

Ida agreed. "I don't think Rogge's promises are being kept, Lillian. It seems to me we are heading toward Europe."

"If we are taken to Europe, I hope we will get to go on to Tanganyika from there," Mother continued. "You know, by now we should have been with Elmer. I wonder how he is getting along. He must be terribly worried. I pray for him all the time." Mother's voice choked with tears.

Ida put her arms around Mother and held her close. "We pray for him, too, Lillian," Ida said lovingly. After a pause, she continued, "Try not to be discouraged. God can bring some good from this terrible experience."

May 13th dawned bright and clear. Rumors were circulating that the *Dresden* would be changing course on this day. Sure enough. At noon the *Dresden* made a right turn and headed due east. That was not good news. We had heard talk that the *Dresden* might run the British Blockade and head for a port in German-occupied France. Now, having made the turn eastward, that route and destination seemed certain.

"Mama, what does British Blockade mean?" Evelyn asked at bedtime. Mother was about to answer when Laurence explained: "That means that, before we get to France, we have to travel through miles and miles of ocean which the British are blocking or guarding. That's why it is called a blockade. The British don't want a German ship to go through. The British are at war with the Germans, you know. So, if the British see the *Dresden*, they will try to stop us and probably sink us." Mother wished Laurence had not added that last sentence, even if it was true.

The new precautions made sense now. Mother thought of the drills we had been having recently; they were repeated until everyone could get to a lifeboat or raft station within two minutes. Poor little Wilfred—he thought the drills were the real thing. He would kick and scream, panic-stricken, making us late in getting to our assigned station. Mother would beg Captain Jaeger to excuse her and Wilfred from the drills, but to no avail. Captain Jaeger was meticulous in his readiness for an attack, with absolutely no exceptions. Even our life jackets had been numbered clearly and registered. We were accustomed to using the jackets as pillows, but now we were instructed to carry the jackets everywhere we went, even to the bathrooms. And there were the small emergency bags, stitched from coarse muslin, each holding a piece of bread and any extra underwear or sweater. We were told to sleep fully dressed, even with our shoes on. Readiness at all times was the order.

Earlier, Laurence had watched big guns being moved into position on the ship's bridge and then hidden by bales of hemp and bags of sand. A new name, *OGNAU*, had been painted in place of *DRESDEN* on the ship's sides. It was obvious that, for some time, the Germans had been planning for this course through the British Blockade. Now it was happening.

Captain Jaeger was taking a tremendous risk, putting the lives of his prisoners in peril. At any hour, day or night, a British warship or a submarine or even a plane might attack the *Dresden*. Captain Jaeger had once told us he would not enter battle with the British. Instead, he said, he would signal that he was carrying more than three hundred noncombatants. However, at another time, he had boasted that he would never let the British take his ship, adding that he could blow it up by throwing a switch on the bridge. Mother shuddered at the thought.

However it might come, death was a very real possibility. Our family's bedtime devotions became especially meaningful, sensing that we might not live to see the next day. As usual, Mother assured us of Jesus' love, but now she also asked, "Are we ready to meet Him, kiddies?" We knew that she meant: "Is there anything that is not right between us?" So, with rather amazing humility and candor, we took turns confessing our wrongdoings aloud and asking one another for forgiveness. Then, being at peace with each other, we asked for God's loving forgiveness. We were ready.

Our devotions ended by singing the prayer hymn "Jesus, Tender Shepherd, Hear Me." The last line was filled with new meaning: "Take me, Lord, at last to heaven, Happy there with Thee to dwell."

Awakening safe and sound in the morning, Mother would greet us by suggesting, "Let us thank God for bringing us safely through the night."

"I already have, Mama," Laurence usually answered.

A new day had come, then another and another, as the *Dresden* steamed through guarded waters. Every hour was filled with tension. Carrying life jackets every minute kept us constantly aware that danger was near. We interrupted our play often to study the sky and ocean, searching for possible danger. Once Laurence and his buddies were so sure they had spotted the periscope of a submarine that they ran excitedly to tell the guard. Seen through binoculars, however, the object proved to be only a large tin can.

One night, a violent storm arose. 'O Lord, please make the waves to cease,' Mother prayed. 'What if a submarine hits us tonight! We'd all be lost. We could never survive in lifeboats in waves like this.' The *Dresden* continued to rock even more, pitching wildly on the huge waves. We could hear tin bowls in the dining room crashing and clattering. Those who slept on the floor rolled around helplessly as the storm raged on and on.

The next day it was said that it had been a freak storm, an unusual wind, blowing from the direction opposite of normal winds. "God spared us, Lillian," Edythe explained. "No submarine could have hit us in the freak storm we had last night." Humbly Mother realized that God had answered prayers, not as she had prayed, but as He knew was best.

Another time an English convoy was spotted in the far distance. Those who had binoculars reported that they saw three warships in a line. Quickly Captain Jaeger turned the *Dresden* and steered into the dazzling sunlight. Cutting engines, the *Dresden* idled, waiting, waiting. Eventually the convoy disappeared over the horizon without incident.

'How like life itself,' Mother thought. 'We are safe only when we rest in God's Sonlight, the true Light.' Mother often expressed faith picturesquely.

And, once again, God spoke through a rainbow. Although only partial, the rainbow was clear and filled with hope. Mother felt God's closeness and love, as if he stepped out of the rift in the cloud to say, "Lo, I am with you always, even to the end."

TWENTY
Hallelujahs and Heartaches

The evening of May 18th brought thrilling news: the men near the front of the ship had sighted lights! It was figured they were lights off Cape Fenisterre, at the northwestern corner of Spain. The wonderful news was relayed to the women's quarters. Sure enough! Mother could see the twinkling glow of lights beckoning. "If we can hold out until midnight, we will be in safe waters," one of the guards explained.

What excitement was stirring! "We are almost there! Praise God! Hallelujah! Hallelujah!" It was hard to sleep that night.

Everyone was eager to get out on deck in the morning. This was the first glimpse of land since leaving Recife, Brazil, on April 9th. Today was May 19th. All day we followed the northern coast of Spain, going east toward France. Part of the time we passed through a narrow body of water with tree-covered hills on either side. After having seen nothing but water for six weeks, we feasted our eyes on the lush greens of trees and vineyards, fishing boats, and picturesque villages. Other scenes were of rough, rocky landscape, with snow-capped mountains in the distance. Land. Beautiful land. It seemed almost too good to be true. Our hearts were nearly bursting with happiness.

Early on May 20th the *Dresden* was piloted into the German-occupied harbor of St. Jean-de-Luz, just inside the western edge of France. Three minesweepers, whose nets dragged up big orange colored mines, went before us. The only mishap was the *Dresden*'s getting stuck on a sand bar. Tugs were summoned to help.

Finally, by mid-afternoon, the *Dresden* dropped anchor in

the harbor, and a little motorboat brought over some German naval officers, smartly dressed in crisp, white uniforms.

In the company of the officers, Captain Jaeger passed by us
prisoners on the deck and said proudly, "Vell, I got you tru all
right."

"Yes, thank you," Mother responded aloud, but in her heart
she knew it was God who had brought us here. The German
officers themselves were amazed the *Dresden* had come
through the Blockade safely, a chance of one in a hundred,
some had said.

Now it was time to get organized to leave the *Dresden*. It did
not take long to pack our few belongings. But Wilfred became restless about something. He was looking here and
there, frantically searching.

"Wilfred, what do you want?" Mother asked.

"My cap, my little red cap. I'm going to see land and
Daddy!"

Her heart nearly breaking, Mother took her little son in her
arms and explained as gently as possible, "Daddy is not here.
This is not Africa. We came to another place."

Poor little Wilfred was absolutely heart-broken. Ever since
the family had left Lindsborg, he had been on his way to
Daddy, wearing his little red cap. His young mind had not
grasped that the sinking had changed plans. He cried and
cried. Mother brushed aside a few tears, too.

Others were weeping, also, for it had just been announced
that only American citizens would be allowed to disembark
now. All others would be taken on to Bordeaux and then to
prison camps.

"Mama, Peter and Wendy have to stay on the *Dresden*,"
Luella reported with concern. Peter and Wendy had been favorite playmates. They were British.

The Mundys walked by, holding each other tightly, knowing
they now had less than an hour together. Pastor Mundy was
Canadian and would be sent to the prison camp, but Mrs.
Mundy was American and would return to their children in
the States. Pastor Mundy's face was flushed with tears; Mrs.

Mundy tried to smile bravely.

Mother's heart ached for the Mundys and the other couples who would soon be separated. Jim Russell would have to say good-bye not only to Carolyn, his wife, but also to their baby Janet.

There were several single men and women heading for the prison camp, too, including the entire group of Catholic priests and teachers, who had been traveling on Canadian passports.

A deep sadness was felt by everyone in saying good-bye, for a deep bond had developed among all of us survivors. We had been through so much together; we were like one big family. Most would probably never see each other again here on earth. Tears flowed as friends and loved ones embraced one final time.

Then it was time to leave. We stepped into the waiting motorboat and faced the shore of German-occupied France.

TWENTY-ONE
Biarritz

Giving a final, tearful glance toward our friends remaining on the *Dresden*, we boarded the buses waiting to take us to Biarritz. As the bus rolled along, Mother gazed out the window, soaking in the beauty of trees, grass, flowers—roses on trellises, daisies, chrysanthemums, asters—blooming so profusely near the foundation of houses or in the gardens. 'If earth can be so beautiful, what must Heaven be like!' she sighed.

Shortly before dusk, the buses pulled up in front of a cluster of small hotels in Biarritz. Once the playground of kings and queens, this little French resort town appeared forlorn and cheerless, bearing the marks of a conquered nation. France had fallen to Germany.

What was the news of the rest of the world? There was a newsboy at the corner. A couple of our men strolled over to see today's paper. What a shock! There, across the front of the paper in big, bold, black letters, was the word "*Zamzam.*" Those who could read French interpreted the rest of the headline and story: the *Zamzam* was declared lost, presumed sunk. There seemed to be no hope of any survivors.

Everyone was astir, thinking of loved ones grieving for us. They need to know we are alive!

With perfect timing, a small car with an American flag pulled up at the hotel area and out bounded a middle-aged man who introduced himself as Henry Waterman, the American Consul at Bordeaux. After a brief exchange of greetings, the attention turned to the newspaper headlines. "I'm sorry, but the same news has been on the radio today, all over the world. You see, it has been six weeks since anyone has heard of the whereabouts of the *Zamzam*, not since you left Brazil. It was normal procedure for the ship's owners to declare it lost," the Consul explained, adding, "The Germans have never announced the sinking."

"But what can we do to let our families know we are alive and well?" everyone seemed to be asking. Mother thought of Dad, of course. Today, he had probably heard that his entire family was lost, presumed to be dead.

"May we cable our loved ones?" V. Eugene asked specifically.

"Not yet. But I will send a cable to the State Department this evening, telling of your safe arrival here," the Consul promised. "That should be in the newspaper headlines and on the radio tomorrow morning. Then, tomorrow night, I will send a second cable listing the names of all the Americans who have arrived here."

"But how soon may we send cables ourselves?" V. Eugene persisted.

"I'm very sorry, but you are not permitted to send any cables or letters until after you have left this occupied area," the Consul responded sympathetically.

After recovering from the initial shock of seeing the headlines, many began to comment, "Just think how wonderful it is that the bad news did not come sooner. There could have been a lapse of several days between the time the *Zamzam* was declared lost and the time we arrived in France. As it has turned out, our loved ones will be grieving only one day. This is more than a coincidence; it is another gift from God."

Mother was so thankful that Dad would learn tomorrow that the family was alive. 'But, heavenly Father, keep him from despair tonight, in these hours of grief, before he learns we are still alive,' she prayed over and over.

The hotels were not ready for us yet; apparently we had arrived in Biarritz one day earlier than expected. Even after room assignments had begun, our family waited and waited. Mother began to wonder if we had been forgotten, but finally we heard the name "Danielson" called. A maid led us to the top floor of one of the little hotels and ushered us into a very small room, made even smaller when a crib was brought in for Lois. "But at least we have a verandah, kiddies. This will be fine." The room had an extra table and a place to wash. Mother felt like a queen!

She wondered, however, if we were going to eat tonight. The younger children were fussing and crying. None of us had eaten since the noon meal of watery soup on the *Dresden*. No wonder we were hungry. Finally, after ten o'clock, it was announced that food was available in the dining hall, which was located down seven flights of steps, and across a narrow street. Biarritz also was blacked out, and we groped our way in total darkness and in rain. Taking Wilfred's little hand, Mother picked up Lois and tried to keep from falling down the steep, dark stairs. She was so thankful when Pastor Hult came along to pick up Wilfred.

A simple, but tasty meal, provided by the Red Cross, awaited us. We feasted on several kinds of bologna and delicious dark bread, plus tea and coffee. We could have more than one serving, too. Contentedly, we returned to our hotel room and quickly fell asleep. After two months on the ocean, we were finally on land again and each one of us sleeping on a real bed.

"I hope we will not be staying long in Biarritz, kiddies," Mother said, "but the Consul said it could take ten days to get new passports and other documents. So be good. Mother is proud of you." We smiled. It was just so good to be on land again and to have decent food—ten days would not be too long.

During our first full day in Biarritz Mother was singled out and summoned to an upper room at the hotel, where a stenographer sat prepared to take down Mother's report verbatim for the State Department's records in Washington, DC. It was suggested that she tell what had happened on the morning of the sinking, April 17th, and anything else she cared to share. Mother tried to tell the story simply, but, even so, it took about thirty minutes. In closing she added, "I hope this incident will not lead to war between Germany and our own United States."

Next order of business was to apply for a new passport, and that necessitated having a family picture taken. Dressing in the best clothing we owned or could borrow, we walked downtown to a small upstairs studio. It was hot, dingy, and not too clean. But the photographer knew his trade; the photo turned out to be quite good. Mother wished she could send a print to Dad, but she knew we could mail nothing from France.

Another matter needing immediate attention was clothing. Our family, like many of the survivors, was still wearing ill-fitting, makeshift outfits. Laurence, for example, was still clad in those drawstring shorts and the blanket cape. The need for clothing came to the attention of local charity organizations, as well as the Friends Committee in Paris. Soon, women began arriving at the hotels, carrying bags of used clothing, kindly trying to outfit us. It was truly an act of generosity, considering the shortages the French citizens themselves were facing.

One woman offered black and white striped trousers for Laurence. The trousers were the right length, but were much too big at the waist. Mother graciously accepted the trousers, then, with needle and thread, took some deep tucks to make a better fit. Laurence was not very pleased about the looks of his new pants, but at least they kept his legs warm.

One afternoon, Laurence was called aside by Mr. Murphy, the journalist and fellow survivor. Holding a brand new, brown suede jacket, Mr. Murphy said, "Laurence, throughout this trip I have admired you very much. You're a fine young man. I want you to have this jacket—it's a gift from me." As Laurence put on the jacket, he beamed with thankfulness. Watching on, Mother's eyes brimmed with tears of pride.

Another day Mother was called to the Consul's makeshift office in the hotel. To Mother's utter surprise, every cent she had deposited with the purser on the *Zamzam* was returned to her! It was not much—a few travelers' checks and sixty-five dollars in cash—but at least it would give a new start.

Mother was a wise and cautious spender. She also knew how much we children would enjoy a treat. Now with a few coins tied in the corner of a hankie in her pocket, she headed off toward the business district, taking Wilfred along with her.

They came upon a bakery. 'I'll surprise the children with each a cupcake,' Mother thought happily. So she stood in a long line, awaiting her turn to make a purchase. Wilfred pressed his nose against the glass case, eager for the grand moment when he would bite into a yummy frosted cupcake. Finally Mother and Wilfred were at the head of the line. "Madam, where is your coupon?" the clerk asked. Mother's heart sank as she realized that the cupcakes were rationed. She had no coupon. She could buy nothing here.

When Wilfred realized he would not be getting the cupcake, he threw himself on the bakery floor and began crying loudly in utter anguish. He was completely crushed. Tenderly, Mother gathered her young son in her arms and carried him from the store. 'How many disappointments can a little boy take?' Mother wondered.

Struggling back toward the hotel, Mother and Wilfred came upon a little shop where ice-cream cones could be bought without a coupon. So they hurried back to the hotel to gather the rest of us, and we nearly raced to the store. The cones were very small and ginger-flavored, but we were thrilled to have them. Our delight was worth every cent the cones had cost, after all the weeks of severe deprivation on the *Dresden*.

Because our hotel room was so small, we spent most of each day outdoors. Mother enjoyed watching us run and play in the park. Even Luella, who had become rather listless on the *Dresden*, seemed to have perked up again. Mother missed the baby buggy; it had gone down on the *Zamzam*. When Lois and Wilfred got too tired to walk, Mother and Laurence carried the two little ones.

Even though the United States was not in the war, the Germans were holding us as "wards" while in France. We were never mistreated, but we were always keenly aware of the presence of guards. Some survivors even feared secret observation by Gestapo police, who might be posing as reporters. We longed for the freedom of not being watched day in and day out. We also noticed the German soldiers doing drills near our hotel, their crisp marching accompanied by rhythmic singing and the clicking of hob-nailed boots hitting the cobblestone street. Biarritz had the feeling of a conquered, occupied city. We sensed sadness in the faces of local residents, and there were hardly any young or middle-aged men; most had gone to war.

We had been ordered not to talk to the local residents. Mother did speak with a woman on the sly, however, and she promised to send word to the woman's husband in Singapore, simply letting him know that his wife and little boy were still alive. Being separated from Dad in wartime circumstances made it natural for Mother to feel for this woman. Mother carefully hid the husband's address in three different places, knowing she might need to discard the slips of paper if searched, hoping that at least one scrap would sneak through unnoticed.

By now, we had been told that all Americans from the *Zamzam* must return to the United States. Mother had hoped to go to Tanganyika from Europe. She missed Dad more than ever. When would we be with him again? Mother knew that God can change 'disappointment' into 'His appointment.' Some good can come from this disruption. So she prayed that God would make use of this disappointing change in some way as an appointment for Him—for His glory.

God answered that prayer unexpectedly. As the story of our family being in the deep water of the South Atlantic reached reporters, they began begging for interviews. Although not allowed to come to the hotel, reporters managed to send messages, asking for Mother to meet them downtown. At first Mother declined. Being shy by nature, Mother simply did not like publicity. Also she did not yet see that telling the story was in keeping with God's plan.

The reporters persisted, and other missionaries offered encouragement: "Don't hesitate, Lillian. Your story is unique—being in the water with the six children and Elmer not being along. God can use your story for His purposes. Go ahead—tell the story."

Gradually, Mother began to realize that God could speak to others through the story. It was God's story, not hers. She was just a channel through which He had shown His great goodness and the power of faith and trust. And now He was appointing her to tell about it.

So, Mother brushed her hair, straightened her dress, and faced the cameras, as she humbly told the story and answered reporters' questions, giving God the praise.

TWENTY-TWO
Free at Last!

"We'll be leaving Biarritz in the morning, Lillian," Edythe announced happily on May 30th. "Be ready for the buses by 9:00." Freedom was only hours away. We could hardly sleep that night.

That excitement was dampened the next morning when we learned that the ambulance drivers were not being allowed to leave. The rest of us, however, reached the border town of Hendaye, France, by mid-morning. No ceremony or celebration announced that we were finally free. We simply transferred from buses to a train and entered Spain.

The train's first stop was San Sebastian. Officials there called us "refugees" as they kindly helped us climb into large trucks bearing big Red Cross emblems. We wondered where we were being taken.

Before long, the trucks pulled up in front of the Maria Christina Hotel. Now the celebrating began! Tables were set with white tablecloths, cloth napkins, porcelain dishes, and silverware. Delicious food was served in one course after another—soup, fish, meat, potatoes, and custard.

After feasting, the hotel's entire fourth floor was offered to us *Zamzam*ers for resting. We were getting comfortable when there was a knock at our hotel room door. A newsman stood there, imploring Mother to tell the story before a movie camera, to be used for newsreels in movie theaters in the United States. "But you must be brief, Mrs. Danielson—about five minutes."

Wondering how to tell the story in such a short time, Mother asked, "Is there something special that you want me to talk about?"

"Give that part about faith," the newsman responded without hesitating. "That's what the world wants to hear."

We children waited and watched, fascinated as the newsman set up his equipment. A few minutes later, on a shaded portico of the hotel, the movie camera rolled as Mother told the story of God's miraculous help. Midway through her presentation, however, Wilfred and Lois broke loose from the care of us older children and raced toward Mother, tugging at her skirt and creating quite a rumpus of background noise. Despite that disruption, the newsman said he thought the movie would still be useable.

Then he had another idea: "Let's film a bit of your son's story, too. And how about your oldest daughter?" So, Laurence and I each took a turn standing before the movie news camera and reported what had happened to our family at the sinking of the *Zamzam* and on the prison ship.

Before long, it was time to board the train again and continue the journey across Spain, toward Portugal. The Red Cross provided boxes of sandwiches, cookies, and fruit. It all tasted so good. When night came, we tried to sleep, but we were too excited. We curled up together on the compartment's only bunk and on a second bed made from luggage. Mother sat up all night, holding Lois in her arms.

We did not sleep well during the next day, either, fascinated with the new scenery, especially the groves of olive trees. We saw hundreds of Germans, too, marching or in cars and wagons, perhaps on their way to the Rock of Gibraltar. War was on the mind of everyone. "It won't be long before United States will be in the war," some suggested.

Throughout the train ride, our family was sought by newsmen who jumped on the train at one stop, took notes quickly during impromptu interviews, and then got off the train at the next stop. Mother hoped they were getting the story straight and, most of all, that they did not omit what she said about giving God the credit for saving us.

About supper time on the second travel day, the train

stopped at the small village of Mangualde. The whole town seemed to be out to greet us. There were speeches of welcome and response, tables decorated with both Portuguese and American flags, and ample food. This was Portugal!

The train pulled into Lisbon on schedule the next morning, June 2nd. We were all escorted to buses and taken to Sintra, about twenty miles away, a historic pleasure resort—truly a welcome haven for tired travelers. Our family eagerly settled in our assigned hotel rooms.

Foremost in Mother's thoughts, however, was to let Dad know that we were well. This was her first opportunity to send word to him since the sinking. Esther Olson's brother Marty was in Tanganyika, too, so together Mother and Esther sent a cable to Dad and Marty: "Nineteen safe Sintra. Are Elmer Marty well? Return America ordered. Elmer return cable. Awaiting passage. Pray without ceasing. Love. Danielson Olson." ("Nineteen" referred to the Augustana group, nineteen in number.)

Late the next afternoon, June 3rd, Ida Norberg tapped on Mother's hotel room door, holding a cablegram from Tanganyika. Ida handed the envelope to Mother but waited nearby, in case the cable carried bad news. Mother's heart was pounding. How was her beloved faring? Mother's fingers trembled as she tore open the envelope. Then her eyes fixed on the message: "Hope all well. Praying for you. Love, Elmer." Mother was profoundly relieved. Mother realized this cable had crossed in transit with the one she had sent yesterday, but this cable certainly conveyed the impression that Dad was holding up. 'Thank you, Father, thank you,' Mother murmured, her eyes filled with tears of joy.

With her mind now at peace, Mother could focus on our stay in Portugal. She was grateful for our hotel accommodations, arranged for by the Red Cross. There was plenty of food. "I am so glad to have potatoes again," Laurence commented contentedly. Mother was happy to see that our gaunt, pinched faces were filling out.

There were many interesting sights in the nearby area. We were awed by the King's and Queen's Palaces on the hillsides outside Sintra. Another excursion was to the art gallery, and then on to the zoo in Lisbon. Little Wilfred was overcome with fascination as he watched the baby hippo playing in a pond. Mother was happy that Wilfred, who had always been attracted to puddles and pools, apparently held no fear of water after his dip in the big, big Atlantic pond.

Mother still had a small amount of cash, and Laurence needed a decent suit. So, Laurence was measured carefully by a tailor in Sintra, and in a few days a blue-gray suit was ready, at a cost of only eleven dollars and ninety-five cents. "May I wear it home?" Laurence asked. "Of course," Mother answered, proud of her young man. At last, he was decently dressed after having to wear the mattress cover, the makeshift shorts, and the striped, tucked trousers for so long.

Local Red Cross officials had noticed that others in our family needed more appropriate clothing, too, and Laurence still needed a belt and shoes that fit. A kind woman from the Red Cross found a few items. Mother resolved she would never forget the help given by the Red Cross.

Mother was still hoping to travel to Africa from Portugal, but the State Department made it final: we must return to the United States.

We would not be with Dad again very soon. We were deeply sorry about that. But, thinking about our non-American friends who had been sent to prison camps, Mother realized we were most fortunate to go back to America—to freedom and abundance.

TWENTY-THREE
Welcome Home

Not being able to go to Africa, *Zamzam*ers were eager to get back home to America. As soon as possible, we were being booked on various passenger ships sailing from Lisbon to America. The first survivors to depart were the twenty-six single women, including Esther Olson and Velura Kinnan, who sailed on June 10th on the S. S. *Mouzinho.* Then eight families, including the Johnsons and the Norbergs, were assigned to the S. S. *Serpa Pinto,* which sailed on June 12th.

Mother was assured our turn would come soon. Pastor Hult was waiting, too. On June 14th the awaited news came: "Be ready in two hours. The bus will take you to the S. S. *Exeter.*" Our few possessions were packed quickly.

Then Mother heard a knock. It must be someone coming to say good-bye. No, it was the maid, holding a cablegram. Cautiously opening it, Mother read, "Cable received. We are well. Praying for you. Rest in God. Cable me from America. Stay there. Kiss kiddies. Yours forever. Danielson." Mother was touched by the loving message from her sweetheart. And also, a load was lifted from her mind. Although she really had no choice in the matter, it seemed easier to leave for America with Dad's support and encouragement.

We could hardly believe how fortunate we were to be traveling on the S. S. *Exeter.* There was no blackout. We were not guarded. Although the ship was quite crowded, with many Jewish refugees fleeing to America, our cabin seemed spacious. We had our own bathroom. Our beds were made up with clean, white sheets and real pillows. We had tasty food. "Kiddies, we must never forget to thank God for these good gifts," Mother reminded us often.

Laurence was eager to earn some spending money, and he had an idea. "Mama, I can set up a shoe-shine stand, if you could lend me money to buy the polish." Mother agreed to the small loan, polish was purchased in the ship's little store, the ship's officer gave permission, and Laurence was soon in business. His customers admired his enterprising spirit and careful work; he did well in his venture right from the start. However, when it was learned that Laurence had been on the *Zamzam*, his business, along with generous tips, reached even greater levels. 'Sonny is certainly deserving,' Mother told herself proudly.

On June 22nd, the S. S. *Exeter* stopped at the Bermuda Islands. Many went ashore, but our family stayed on board. Laurence turned eleven that day. Unlike the birthdays of Mother and myself on the *Dresden*, this time we celebrated with cake and ice cream. Bit by bit, it seemed life was returning to normal, even while still far from home.

Before the ship left the harbor at Bermuda, Mother sent a cable to Dad's family in Meriden, Connecticut: "Leaving tonight, arriving New York Tuesday noon." It was hard to believe the journey was nearing an end.

It was the early hours of June 24th. The ship's horn was blowing. 'Oh dear, what's happening?' Mother wondered sleepily, the frightening memory of April 17th never far from her consciousness. Hurriedly looking out on deck, Mother realized gratefully, 'It's only the fog horn.'

Mother lay down in her bunk again, but she was too excited to go back to sleep. In a few more hours, the S. S. *Exeter* would be docking in the New York harbor.

It was still hazy as the New York skyline came into view. Though not lighted, the Statue of Liberty seemed more beautiful than ever, welcoming home weary travelers. For Mother, the word "home" had never seemed so good.

As the ship docked, we saw Dr. Swanson of the Mission Board and Uncle Irving there to meet us. They waved, and we waved back, eager to join them.

Before we knew what was happening, reporters and photographers were swarming around us, asking questions, begging for pictures. Mother did her best to respond to the newsmen. Again and again, she emphasized that it was God alone who had brought us safely through the sinking of the *Zamzam* and the month on the prison ship.

We children were impatient. We wanted to leave. Smiles turned into frowns as we posed for one picture after another. "Kiddies, please cooperate just a little longer. We'll soon be through," Mother promised gently.

Finally, the photographers and reporters left us. Then Mother picked up Lois, took Wilfred by the hand, and, with Luella clinging to her skirt and Laurence, Evelyn, and myself following closely, this brave and humble heroine, our mother, walked down the gangplank.

Uncle Irv and Dr. Swanson embraced us warmly, their tears saying more than words at a time like this. Tears of gratitude. Tears of joy. Tears of marvel. So much had happened to our family since we had left New York three months earlier. If even one child had been lost or maimed, the homecoming would have been different. But here we were, all healthy and well. Only Dad was missing.

Dr. Swanson inquired about our plans for returning to Kansas and also shared news about others in the Augustana group. We were glad to hear that Pastor Hult would be arriving in New York on the 30th of June.

Soon we eagerly climbed into Uncle Irv's waiting car. In less than two hours, we were at Grandma Danielson's home in Meriden, Connecticut. Grandma wept and wept as she hugged us, one by one. "You are so courageous, Lillian," we heard Grandma say through her tears.

We wondered how Grandma had gotten the news of the sinking. "I heard it on the radio on May 19th. It was in the newspaper, too," she told us. "It was such a shock. I just could not believe you were all gone. I prayed and prayed that God had spared you somehow. And my heart broke thinking about dear Elmer, alone in Tanganyika." Grandma wiped her eyes and continued, "And then, the very next day, the morning news said you were in France. God is so good. So good."

"But you know how I really learned what had happened—I mean, what had happened to you folks—and that you were all right?" Grandma was saying. She put her arm around me and continued, "I saw you, Eleanor, on a newsreel at the movie theater. Yes, there you stood, as big as real life, and you told how the *Zamzam* had been shelled and you had all been in the water. And you said you had been on the prison ship a month, but you were all fine. I'll never, never forget it." We remembered how the newsreel had been filmed in San Sebastian, Spain, at the hotel. Mother was rather surprised that Grandma had seen the newsreel, since Grandma did not go to the movie theater. However, when a friend had told Grandma about the newsreel, she had hurried to the theater and even stayed for a second showing.

After a few days of resting and celebrating with relatives and friends in Connecticut and Massachusetts, we left for Kansas. On the train and in depots it was not uncommon to be recognized as "that family that was in the ocean." We felt self-conscious and embarrassed by the attention. Newsmen still asked for interviews and pictures. What bothered Mother most was the fact that newspaper stories had inaccuracies, some rather glaring. Some reports said that the *Zamzam* had been torpedoed. Another paper said that our family had been machine-gunned in the water. The most disturbing untruth claimed that Mother was expecting another baby.

The trip back to Kansas was by way of Chicago, where we spent the weekend visiting friends. Mother was asked to speak at a Sunday evening gathering at Messiah Church, in the Austin neighborhood. For nearly two hours, an overflow audience sat enthralled as Mother told the *Zamzam* story. There was hardly a dry eye. We children took part, too, singing choruses we had learned on the *Dresden*, including our favorite, "Safe Am I."

Another stop on our way back to Lindsborg was in Kansas

City, where we visited our cousin. A neighbor tipped off local newspapers, which resulted in more interviews. Of course, newspapers carried stories of other survivors, too, including the release of the ambulance drivers.

We were so eager to be back in our own home in Lindsborg. But first, we visited Mother's childhood home near Chanute, Kansas.

At last, we headed for Lindsborg. Uncle Gust helped us children climb into the back of his old truck. The sides of the truck bed had been reinforced by a wooden frame, and an overhead tarp protected us from the scorching July sun. Mother rode in the cab beside Uncle Gust.

As the truck started down the driveway at Uncle Gust's farm, Mother turned to look at us. 'They do look like refugees,' she thought. Suddenly, she was overcome with emotion. 'My precious children. They have been on such a dangerous journey, enduring so much together. They have been so brave. What a miracle that we are all alive. Thank you, Father. Thank you.' Tears trickled down Mother's cheeks. Tenderly Uncle Gust put his arm around his little sister.

We arrived back in Lindsborg on July 14th, almost exactly four months after we had left in March. Eagerly, we crawled out of the truck and bounded into the house. Before long Uncle Gust and Laurence pulled pieces of furniture from the storage bedroom and put things in place. Friends came over with groceries and invitations for meals. Young friends came over to see us playmates again.

At bedtime, Evelyn observed, "Everyone acts like we are different, like we are famous now. But I feel just the same." Laurence and I echoed Evelyn's feelings. We all yearned for ordinary, normal life.

But life could not be completely normal, for someone very special was missing. Luella expressed it in her sweet way, "I miss Daddy, and I know he misses us." She threw her arms around Mother and gave her a tender kiss.

"I miss Daddy, too, dear," Mother murmured softly, wiping away a tear. "God has been so good to bring us back safely.

Kiddies, let us never forget to thank and praise Him, even when we are missing Daddy. I feel we have been 'saved to serve' in whatever way God needs to use our family. I am sure God will bring us all together again someday."

TWENTY-FOUR
Saved to Serve

How had Dad heard the news of the sinking? How was he doing? Mother longed to know more details from Dad and also to read his words of tenderness and love. The last letter from Dad had been written the previous November.

Finally, the letters began to come. Even though they took more than six weeks to arrive, they brought Dad close again.

One letter also answered the questions which had been haunting Mother. With tears flowing, she read Dad's lines over and over again. The month of May had been sheer agony for him. For days, he had wondered why there had been no news from his beloved; he had expected a letter from Capetown. As the date for the family to arrive in Mombasa had come and gone, and there had been absolutely no word from anyone in the *Zamzam* group, Dad's concern had turned to anxiety. 'But Father, they are in Your care. Bring them here safely in Your time,' he had prayed over and over.

On May 19th, Africa time, Dad had been called to the bedside of a young Scottish miner, dying of blackwater fever. Dad had sat with the young man all night. At dawn the next day, missionary doctor Stan Moris arrived unexpectedly, and, taking Dad by the arm, tearfully broke the news: "The *Zamzam* has been reported long overdue over last night's radio, and it is feared it has been sunk by enemy action."

Moment by moment, the terrible news sank into Dad's consciousness. His world became nothing but darkness as grief overcame him. Going to the home of missionary friends, he tried to get more news by way of the radio. But there was none. The agony of loss and uncertainty was almost too much to bear.

The following morning, the young miner died. Being the only pastor in the area, Dad needed to conduct the funeral service, held later that same day. In the depths of sorrow himself, Dad prepared a sermon of comfort and hope, for himself as much as for the young man's mourners.

Shortly before the service was to begin, someone hurried to Dad with the wonderful news that it had just been announced on the radio that Americans from the *Zamzam* were alive and had arrived in France. Unimaginable relief and joy swept over Elmer. 'But could I dance for joy at a funeral?' That night, he heard the news again on a radio broadcast.

After the initial relief, however, Dad worried. 'Are Lillian and the children well? What have they been through? It is too much to think that all seven of them have survived without some injuries.'

Even after our family's return to Lindsborg in July, it took several letters and photographs to convince Dad that, yes, the whole family was doing fine. The only obvious mark of the *Zamzam* trauma was sensitivity to sudden noises, for Mother especially.

The United States entered the war that December 1941. That resulted in even fewer missionaries being able to travel to overseas fields. The need for Dad to stay on in the work in Tanganyika remained critical. Dad wrestled in his soul as never before. 'I can never thank God enough for all His goodness to us. He helped spare my sweetheart and precious kiddies. The least I can do is to continue serving here, if Lillian and the children can manage alone in Lindsborg. But how does she feel about it? Should I return to the States or stay in Tanganyika at this time? Father, show me Your will.'

After several days of praying, Dad sat down at his desk, hesitantly put a sheet of paper in his old typewriter, and began to pour out his thoughts and questions in a letter to Mother and us children.

Mother was home alone when the letter arrived. Her fingers

trembled as she gently opened the envelope. Somehow she sensed it bore a message of deep importance. Slowly and silently, she read Dad's lines. As she read, she could feel how torn he was between yearning to be back in the States with the family and his commitment to the mission work overseas.

Naturally, Mother considered her own situation. She ached to be in her sweetheart's arms again and to have him beside her, raising the children. But again and again, it was as if God was telling her, 'Elmer is still greatly needed in Tanganyika.' Mother shared the letter with us. For several days, we talked and prayed about Dad's question. The little children could not understand, but we older ones seemed to feel God had a special purpose for Dad in Africa at this time. Furthermore, we felt we had been "saved to serve," even if it meant family separation for a while longer. Sometimes sacrifice was part of being Jesus' followers. So Mother sent the cable: "We're all well. Stay Africa. Come in God's time. God bless and use you. Love, Danielsons." The matter was settled. Mother was at peace about it.

Dad, too, felt the decision was in keeping with God's will. He tried to accept it and adjust. As superintendent of all the Lutheran missions of Tanganyika, Dad's schedule was filled with meetings and traveling throughout the country. Then he would come home alone to the little mission house at Wembere, where the beds had been ready to welcome his precious family. At times, his heart was ready to burst with loneliness as he ached for his sweetheart and kiddies. Although he was well loved by his African co-workers, there was a certain feeling of isolation in being the only missionary at Wembere.

It was war—not God—that had brought about this separation. War is terrible! Thousands of other families were facing separation because of war, and some husbands and dads were giving their very lives in combat. Compared to them, Dad reasoned, his situation was mild, his sacrifice small.

Mother's life in Lindsborg was quite different from Dad's circumstance. We six growing children not only gave Mother some companionship and generous expressions of love, but our activities in school, church, music lessons, sports, paper routes, chores, and play kept Mother on the run. Each day was fulfilled to overflowing. In addition, caring friends and a loving community surrounded Mother.

Mother was also in great demand as a speaker, telling the *Zamzam* story in many Kansas towns and traveling even to other states. When the speaking engagements were nearby, some of us children accompanied Mother, delighting audiences by modeling replica life jackets and singing the choruses learned on the *Dresden*. Mother was a gifted, natural storyteller. Her sincerity, as well as the unusual drama of the story itself, captivated audiences. It was not unusual for Mother to speak for nearly two hours, keeping her listeners spellbound.

It was not easy for Mother to travel. We had no car, so she had to depend on bus or train service. She felt also hesitant about leaving us children at home, usually under a friend's supervision. Mother would have preferred to stay home.

However, deep in her heart Mother sensed God's call to witness by telling the story. Again and again, she prayed that God would use the story for His purposes. "It was God who brought us through safely. It was not anything we did. God did it all. To Him belongs the thanks and praise," she would say as she ended yet another presentation and wearily headed toward home.

TWENTY-FIVE
Reunited

Months passed. Slowly the months rolled into years. Lois was no longer thought of as the family baby; she was an active preschooler. Laurence had become a lanky teen-ager. Pictures and letters had become the tangible link between our family in Lindsborg and Dad in Tanganyika. Every week, usually on Sunday afternoons, Mother would put her old manual type-writer on the dining room table. Her fingers flying on the keys, she would type as we children took turns dictating letters to our absent Daddy.

Letters from Dad came quite regularly, too. As Mother read them aloud, tears welled. We children knew she missed Dad. Luella still gave an extra kiss at bedtime, adding, "That one is from Daddy." As a family, we talked and prayed often for God's leading about when Dad should return to the States. We knew the separation was meant to be only temporary.

In the summer of 1944, Dad wrote that it seemed the way was becoming clear for him to leave. Others were now able to take over the leadership he had been giving. In addition, he admitted, his loneliness was becoming almost unbearable. He felt it was God's time now to come home.

A later letter indicated Dad was making travel plans. Since this was still wartime, and letters were being censored, he dared not tell what his travel plans would be. Letters became scarcer and then stopped. Mother knew her beloved was on the way home.

Eventually, on October 28th, 1944, a telegram came. Dad had arrived in Miami, Florida! He would be home soon! First, he needed to report to church headquarters in New York

City, and, from New York, he would briefly visit his ailing
mother in nearby Connecticut. Then he would head toward
Kansas. Mother could hardly believe it was happening. It had
been nearly four-and-a-half years since Dad had left.

A telegram came from Chicago on Saturday afternoon, November 4th. "Will arrive McPherson tomorrow afternoon at
2:35. Love, Daddy." Mother's heart beat wildly. Trying to
speak calmly, she called Pastor Claypool to share the good
news and also ask if he would drive the family to meet the
train in McPherson. He said "yes."

As our family gathered in our home for lunch that Sunday,
there was a sense of quiet excitement. Nobody cared to talk,
and nobody seemed hungry. Awkwardly we older children
brushed aside tears now and then, thinking of what was about
to happen. When Pastor Claypool's car arrived, Mother and
all of us children solemnly piled in and hardly said a word
during the fourteen miles to McPherson. Pastor Claypool
seemed to understand.

Reaching the train station platform, we all stood quietly, listening, waiting, and wondering. Finally, we heard the train's
whistle. And there came the train, slowly rounding the curve.
The brakes were grinding to a stop. Mother was battling between tears and smiles. She could not keep from quivering.

Then Dad stepped down from the train, wearing a gray
straw hat and a tan topcoat over his blue suit. Mother stepped
forward to embrace her husband. The two of them stood
there, nestled in each other's arms, tears trickling down their
cheeks. We children watched, some of us in tears, others too
young to comprehend the depth of this moment.

Finally, Dad turned to us and gave each of us a long, long
hug. For years he had longed to hold his family again, close to
his loving heart. Now his prayers were being answered.

As we rode back to Lindsborg, Dad kept looking at us, finding it hard to believe that the tall young man beside him was
Laurence, who was just a boy of ten when he had left. And
this charming little five-year-old blonde with twinkling brown
eyes was the baby he had left behind. All six of us had grown

and changed more than Dad could grasp. As for Mother, she was more beautiful than ever before, her face radiant with love and inner joy. Dad's arm tightened around Mother again. 'Is this really happening?' he kept asking himself.

Mother, too, was filled with indescribable joy. Scenes flashed through Mother's mind, remembering times when she had wondered if she would ever see her sweetheart again— the shelling, being in the ocean, the night on the raider, the long days and nights on the prison ship, all the years since then. And now Dad was beside her again.

Before long the car stopped in front of our home. We posed for a picture.

Then, our hearts overflowing with thanks, Mother, Dad, and we six children—Laurence, Eleanor, Evelyn, Luella, Wilfred, and Lois—walked into our little home in Lindsborg, reunited again as a complete family. Praise be to God!

Epilogue

God's goodness has continued to bless our family through all the years. Reunions have followed farewells, joy has flowed through serving, and peace has filled the empty places.

At the close of this story, in late 1944, we had just been reunited as a complete family. After a furlough, Mother, Dad, and the three younger children journeyed to Africa for the next term of service. We three older children remained in Lindsborg, with Einar and Betty Jaderborg as our housemates. Only Wilfred and Lois were with our parents in Tanzania during our parents' next term of service. Finally, Mother and Dad returned to Africa alone, serving overseas until their retirement in 1968.

Meanwhile, Lindsborg continued as home for us children. We are indebted to the whole community for the care and kindness that nurtured us. All six of us graduated, in turn, from Bethany College in Lindsborg, married, and established our own homes and careers.

Laurence worked as a coach and teacher before becoming a high school administrator in Colorado. Most of my adult years have been spent in Illinois. After teaching school for two years, I married Phil Nelson and shared his ministry as a pastor's wife. Phil's sudden death in 1985 eventually led to my marriage to Carl, a widowed pastor. Evelyn worked as a nurse both in Liberia and in the United States, and now she lives in California. Luella became an elementary schoolteacher in South Dakota, but she has retired in Arkansas. Wilfred is employed by the federal government as a librarian in Washington, DC. After pioneering as a social worker in Dar es Salaam, Tanzania, Lois has served with the Lutheran Social Services in Kansas.

After our parents retired, we children often gathered in Lindsborg, together with our own families. Dad's schedule as interim pastor, chaplain, writer, and speaker remained quite busy, but he always welcomed us with open arms. We sensed that Mother could never forget the awesome experience of April 17, 1941. As she looked at us gathered around the dining room table, she often thought back to our cold, soaking plunge in the deep Atlantic, marveling at God's saving goodness. Nearly every year for *Zamzam* Day, she wrote a letter of her reflections on that fateful day.

We were blessed to have Mother and Dad with us for many years. Cancer caused Dad's death in 1994. One year later, a week after she had celebrated her 96th birthday, Mother's heart failed, and she joined Dad in that great reunion in heaven.

This book tells about the *Zamzam* experience as it affected our family. Each survivor, however, has her or his own remarkable story to tell. At the *Zamzam* reunions held since 1991, other survivors have shared their personal stories and have become reacquainted with one another. Newsletters keep all of us in touch between reunions. This renewed bond of friendship and fellowship has been another gift of God's graciousness.

"Bless the Lord, O my soul, and forget not all His benefits." (Psalm 103:2)

Eleanor Anderson

PICTURES

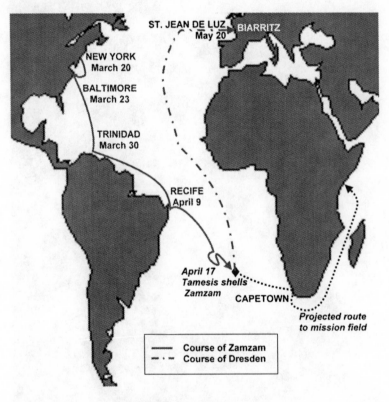

Map
(Prepared by David Trobisch)

Lillian Danielson 1927.
(Courtesy Anderson Family Archive)

Rev. Elmer R. Danielson 1928.
(Courtesy Anderson Family Archive)

Rev. Ralph Hult.
(Courtesy Ingrid Youngdale Family Archive)

A lifeboat filled with passengers and crew from the *Zamzam*
pulls away from the listing ship.
(Photo courtesy Life Magazine. Copyright 1941 Time Inc. All Rights Reserved.)

Damage on the *Zamzam*.
(Photo courtesy Life Magazine. Copyright 1941 Time Inc. All Rights Reserved.)

Passengers and crew climb down a ladder. The lifeboat
seems already loaded to capacity.
(Photo courtesy Life Magazine. Copyright 1941 Time Inc. All Rights Reserved.)

Germans are taking off baggage and provisions from the *Zamzam.*
(Photo courtesy Life Magazine. Copyright 1941 Time Inc. All Rights Reserved.)

Passengers from the *Zamzam* watch the sinking from the deck of the
Tamesis (*Atlantis*). Charges were set off by time fuses.
(Photo courtesy Life Magazine. Copyright 1941 Time Inc. All Rights Reserved.)

The German raider *Atlantis*, disguised under the Norwegian name *Tamesis*.
(Photo courtesy Life Magazine. Copyright 1941 Time Inc. All Rights Reserved.)

Men from the *Zamzam* are briefed by the *Dresden*'s Captain Jaeger, wearing
a dark cap. *Zamzam*'s Captain Smith wears a white cap.
(Photo courtesy Life Magazine. Copyright 1941 Time Inc. All Rights Reserved.)

Meeting of Husbands and Wives for two hours each
morning on the deck of the *Dresden*.
(Photo courtesy Life Magazine. Copyright 1941 Time Inc. All Rights Reserved.)

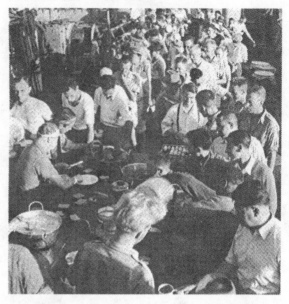

Male prisoners line up for food on the *Dresden*.
(Photo courtesy Life Magazine. Copyright 1941 Time Inc. All Rights Reserved.)

Men in the cargo hold of the *Dresden*. They were allowed on
deck only at the permission of the German guard.
(Photo courtesy Life Magazine. Copyright 1941 Time Inc. All Rights Reserved.)

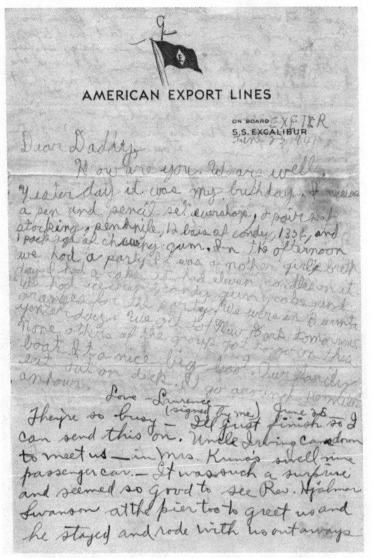

Letter (June 23, 1941) from Laurence to his father
en route from Lisbon to New York.
(Courtesy Anderson Family Archive)

Cablegram sent from Portugal to Tanganyika.
(Courtesy Anderson Family Archive)

Back row: Velura Kinnan, Esther Olson, Marie Norberg, Einar Norberg,
Ida Norberg, V. Eugene Johnson, Edythe Johnson, Hjalmar Swanson.
Front row: Ruth Norberg, Carl Norberg, Vic Johnson with David
Johnson.

Mrs. Danielson and her six children (Eleanor with cap on) arriving in
New York from Lisbon, Portugal aboard the S.S. *Exeter*.
(Copyright New York Times, June 25, 1941)

Lillian Danielson and her children (Eleanor, Laurence, Wilfred, Luella,
Lois, and Evelyn) arrive in New York more than two months after the
sinking of the *Zamzam*.
(Copyright The New York Times, 1941)

July 1941. The last leg of an epic 10,000 mile journey. The ride from Vilas
to Lindsborg in the pick-up truck of Lillian Danielson's brother, Gust.
Luella, Evelyn, Eleanor, Lois against Laurence's arm.
Wilfred behind Laurence.
(Courtesy Anderson Family Archive)

The Danielson family reunited at last. The picture was taken soon after
Elmer Danielson arrived in Lindsborg, Kansas, joining his family more
than 3 ½ years after the sinking of the *Zamzam*.
(Courtesy Anderson Family Archive)

Mrs. Danielson and her 6 children in 1991. Back row: Laurence, Eleanor, Evelyn. Front row: Wilfred, Lillian, Luella, Lois.
(Courtesy Anderson Family Archive)

Eleanor Anderson.

Quiet Waters Publications

Bolivar MO 65613-0034
www.quietwaterspub.com:

On Our Way Rejoicing

By Ingrid Trobisch
Ralph Hult had embarked on the ill-fated *Zamzam* as well. After returning to the US he set out for Tanzania the following year where he died unexpectedly. His daughter, Ingrid Trobisch, tells the story of what happens when God takes away the father of ten children. A whole family is called to service and sent into the world. The story surges with movement, partings and reunion, sorrows and joys, adventure and romance, shining courage, and above all, the warm love that knits together a large Christian family.
ISBN 0-9663966-2-6

Daktari Yohana

By John Hult
These captivating stories describe the experiences of a missionary doctor in Tanzania, East Africa. If you love Africa, you will enjoy this book.
ISBN 0-9663966-5-0

I Married You

By Walter Trobisch
Set in a large African city, this story covers only four days in the life of Walter and Ingrid Trobisch. Nothing in this book is fiction. All the stories have really happened. The people involved are still living today. The direct, sensitive, and compassionate narrative presents Christian marriage as a dynamic triangle. ISBN 0-9663966-6-9

I Loved A Girl

By Walter Trobisch

'Last Friday, I loved a girl – or as you would put it, I committed adultery.' This deeply moving story of a young African couple has become a worldwide classic with its frank answers to frank questions about sex and love. Its tremendous success led Walter and Ingrid Trobisch to leave their missionary post in Cameroun and start an international ministry as marriage and family counselors.

ISBN 0-9663966-0-X

The Adventures Of Pumpelhoober

By David Trobisch, illustrated by Eva Bruchmann

"In Austria they call someone who has a lot of bad luck, 'Pumpelhoober'. I, too, often have bad luck," nine year old David explains his nickname. This humorous children's book tells the story of the Trobisch family in Africa from the perspective of a child.

ISBN 0-9663966-4-2

Touched by the African Soul

Compiled by Gloria Cunningham & Lois Okerstrom

A collection of short stories, written by sixty-two missionary women who recall their adventuresome years in Tanzania. The stories tell of personal experiences of the writers and give insight into the culture and Christian faith of the Tanzanian people among whom they lived and worked.

ISBN 0-9663966-9-3

Passport to Borneo

By Adeline Lundquist Hult

In 1951 the author was called as a missionary teacher to work with a Chinese church in British North Borneo. Her experiences of living abroad for the first time, the joys, frustrations, and adaptations necessary to cope with life in a multi-cultural colony, are all graphically portrayed in a story of personal relationships and human interest.

ISBN 1-931475-03-2

Singing I Go

By Beryl Ramsey Sand

She heard the Spirit's call to serve as a missionary at the age of fifteen. Ten years later, in May of 1944 and in the midst of World War II, Beryl arrived in Africa. She worked as a nurse, as a literacy teacher, and she assisted in writing the first Bible teaching material in the Gbaya language. In this book Beryl chronicles her life through her memories and letters.

ISBN 1-931475-02-4